The Evolution of Brazil
compared with that of
Spanish and Anglo-Saxon America

BY

MANOEL DE OLIVEIRA LIMA

Edited with Introduction and Notes
BY
PERCY ALVIN MARTIN

Foreword
BY
NATHALIA HENRICH

The Catholic University
of America Press

Originally published by Stanford University Press, 1914

Foreword © 2019 The Catholic University of America Press
All rights reserved

ISBN 978-0-8132-3266-9

FOREWORD TO THE PAPERBACK EDITION

Percy Alvin Martin, a pioneer historian of Latin America, wrote in the preface of the first edition of this book that Manoel de Oliveira Lima would need no introduction for those who were familiar with the field. More than a hundred years later, that statement is not quite accurate anymore. Not in his native Brazil, where he has been rediscovered more recently, and certainly not in the United States, his final home.

Hailed as the "Intellectual Ambassador of Brazil", Oliveira Lima (1867, Recife, Brazil-1928, Washington, D.C.) was a man of letters and member of numerous learned societies around the world who excelled in his many professional roles as a historian, journalist, professor, publicist, writer, and diplomat. During his lifetime, he was one of the most prominent scholars in the field of Latin American Studies, recognized for his scholarship and sharp tongue - or pen. His life did not lack controversy and the number of enemies he made was only matched by the admirers he conquered. The impact on his career was felt deeply.

Many reasons led to his near erasure of the canon of early Latin-Americanists in the United States, where he lived the last years of his life in a "voluntary exile" after a contentious retirement from the diplomatic corps. One of them, maybe the most relevant, is the scarce number of his works published here. The six lectures that constitute this book were imparted in the Fall of 1912 at Stanford University and written originally in English (they were later translated and published in Portuguese and Spanish). Although there are numerous articles in journals, magazines and newspapers, *The Evolution of Brazil compared with that of Spanish and Anglo-Saxon America*, published in 1914, remains to this day the only book by Oliveira Lima in English. Therefore, it is appropriate timing for this work to be brought back to light in a new edition.

As many centenary pieces of scholarship, this has not passed unscathed the test of time. The mere use of the word evolution in the title can be enough to make historians and social scientists cringe. There is room for debate over the use of concepts such as conquest and discovery, not to mention the idea of the existence of "racial harmony" in Brazil. The text still carries the weight of now debunked racial theories, heavily influenced by Social Darwinism. The concept of race itself, used as an interpretative tool aimed to support a "cultural" analysis of national identities, is pervasive. Nevertheless, the innovative use of a comparative approach and sound use of primary sources gathered in painstaking archival research worldwide is still worth the reading. Furthermore, it constitutes an important source in the history of the field of Latin American studies in the country.

This edition by The Catholic University of America Press represents an effort to introduce Manoel de Oliveira Lima to a new generation of American scholars. The circumstance is only fitting since his life and work is inextricably linked to Catholic University. It was through the donation of his colossal personal library and personal papers more than a century ago that he planted the seeds for the Oliveira Lima Library, praised today as one of the finest Luso-Brazilian collections in the world. In his long life as a diplomat, he was always a fierce advocate for intellectual exchange among countries as a tool to nurture understanding and prosperity. The Oliveira Lima Library is the embodiment of his views.

My hope is that this edition will prompt a renewed interest in the life and works of an extraordinary man. A man who believed that knowledge was the most effective tool to build bridges, bring countries together, and promote peace. More importantly, a man who devoted his life to this cause.

NATHALIA HENRICH, PHD   Director of The Oliveira Lima Library
                             at The Catholic University of America

CONTENTS

	PAGE
INTRODUCTION	9

LECTURE I.

The conquest of America.—Religious defence of the native element.—Indians and negroes.—The color problem and the discrimination against the colonists.—The institution of slavery and the conditions of political independence in the Spanish and Portuguese colonies, affecting diversely the abolition of slavery.—The first Spanish American civil war and the verdict of history in regard to it.—The social organization in the possessions of the New World.—The Indians and the clergy.—The part taken by the Jesuits.—The fusion of the races and the neo-European product.—Causes of the separation: disregard of nationality and economic exploitation.—Monopolies and prohibitions.—Spiritual tutelage and emancipation.—Historical reasons for the Catholic intolerance.—Intellectual revival of the Iberian Peninsula during the Spanish reign of Charles III, and under the Portuguese dictatorship of the Marquis de Pombal.—Influence of this revival in the colonies. . . . 16

LECTURE II.

European ideas brought over the sea by contraband books and native travelers.—Intercourse between mother-country and colony.—The intellectual progress of the New World of Latin America before its political emancipation.—Comparison with the progress of the British possessions.—The race, environment, and period.—The race problem in America.—Traditional sympathy felt in Latin America for the inferior races.—State of the colonial culture in the Iberian and Anglo-Saxon sections.—Territorial conquests of Portuguese and Spaniards.—The political unit: the municipal chambers and *cabildos*.—Their conception and realization in the colonies and their significance in the mother-countries of Europe.—The *Cabildo* of Montevideo and the part it took in the Revolution.—The municipal chambers of Brazil and Independence.—The political and social reconstruction of the new countries.—Education and charity.—Characteristics of colonial education.—The lack of political education in Latin America.—The general characteristics of particularism and the American conception of federalism. . . 36

LECTURE III.

Origin of the federative principle.—Local government and administrative centralization in Portuguese and Spanish America: Their different aspects.—Lack of uniformity in colonial legislation.—Viceroys and *Audiencias*.—Union through confederation in the three Americas.—

Schemes of American royalties: Aranda, Pitt and Chateaubriand.—The monarchical idea in Latin America and its moral effect.—The first Monroe Doctrine.—Franco-British rivalries in the course of the eighteenth and nineteenth centuries.—Napoleon and the British interests in the New World.—Monarchical possibilities in Buenos Aires, Mexico, and Colombia.—Pitiable rôle of Ferdinand VII.—Iturbide, Bolívar, and San Martin.—European or creole dynasties.—Historical function of the Brazilian Empire.—The moderate minds in the colonies and liberal ideas in Spain.—Precedents for the idea of separation.—The traditional discontent, the genesis of the patriotic instinct, and the personal tie between the sovereign and his possessions in America. . . . 55

LECTURE IV.

Representative types in the struggle for the independence of the New World.—The Mexican curate Hidalgo and the Latin American clergy, partisans of national independence.—The Brazilian priests in the revolution, in the Constituent Assembly and in the government.—Temporary union of the aristocratic, religious and popular elements.—The creole royalty of Iturbide and the imperialistic jacobinism of Bolívar.—The conservative and the revolutionary elements in the new political societies.—José Bonifacio, Dom Pedro and Brazilian emancipation.—Bolívar's political psychology and its historical parallel with that of San Martin.—Their double sketch in the light of sociology, by F. Garcia Calderon.—Their antagonistic temperaments and different education.—Federation applied, and the international ideal of Bolívar: Solidarity, mediation, arbitration and territorial integrity.—The pact of Panama and the abstention of the United States.—Bolívar's nationalism, his generosity.—Nativism of the subsequent *libertadores;* more in harmony with the environment.—Melancholy destiny of the superior men of the Independence and of their patriotic work.—Advent of the anarchic element, premature political decadence, and dawn of regeneration. . . . 74

LECTURE V.

The work of neo-Latin emancipation and the Iberian-American element.—Andres Bello and Mariano Moreno, types of superior colonial intellects.—The books which San Martin and Bolívar read.—Critical sense of Bolívar.—The poem *Junin,* by Olmedo.—Constituent assemblies and constitutions.—The "Middle Ages" of the new Spanish-Portuguese world.—Its first intellectual currents.—The liberal ideas of the generation of the Independence and the part taken by the colonial representatives in the Cortes of Cadiz and Lisbon.—Character of the literature of the new countries.—Heroic poetry and the Indianist school.—The tradition of the mother-tongue among the neo-Spanish peoples.—The cult of the Past.—French influence in literature and politics.—The eclecticism of Cousin and the Positivist training.—Effect of English and German philosophies.—European Idealism in America.—Science and mental speculation.—Traditionalism and Modernism. . . . 94

LECTURE VI.

Moral integration produced by the fusion of the races, the condition of social equilibrium.—The historic episode of Bolívar and Pétion.—Disadvantages of intermarriage, which gives rise to a great difference in ideals.—Political unrest of Latin America, formerly the hope of the European democracy.—Causes of the revolutionary disturbances.—The anarchical and conservative elements in the Iberian societies of the New World.—Bolívar's conception and its realization in Brazil.—Strength of traditionalism.—Historic function of the Brazilian Monarchy.—Federation and the rule of dictators.—Private initiative and the work of education and moralization.—Liberty and tyranny.—Troubles in the evolutionary march of the peoples across the sea.—Lack of harmony between the theory and practice, between the régime and the people.—The Brazilian oligarchy during the empíre and its mission.—Political regeneration through social education and economic development.—Mariano Moreno and Dom John VI.—Industrialism and the emancipation of the people.—Violence and culture.—Qualities, services and glories of Latin America.—The American conscience and Pan-Americanism.—America for humanity. 112

Notes on Lecture I. 130

Notes on Lecture II. 136

Notes on Lecture III. 140

Notes on Lecture IV. 144

Notes on Lecture V. 151

Notes on Lecture VI. 156

INTRODUCTION

THE six lectures included in the present volume were delivered at Leland Stanford Junior University in the autumn of 1912 by Dr. OLIVEIRA LIMA under the auspices of the Department of History. To those familiar with the recent contributions of Latin America and, more especially, Brazil, in the field of historical scholarship the distinguished author of these lectures needs no introduction; as historian, essayist and diplomat, he has won a commanding place in the intellectual activities of contemporary Brazil; as a tireless investigator and productive scholar, he has done much to raise the study of South American History to a dignity and importance it had never previously enjoyed.

Manoel de Oliveira Lima was born in Pernambuco, Brazil, December 25, 1865. At the age of twenty he received the degree of Doctor of Philosophy and Letters at the University of Lisbon; two years later he embarked upon a diplomatic career of unusual fruitfulness. From 1892 to 1900 he was attaché to the Brazilian embassies at Berlin, Washington and London. In 1901 he was appointed minister to Japan; from 1902 to 1913 he represented Brazil in a similar capacity in Peru, Venezuela, Sweden and Belgium, and on various occasions he was intrusted with important foreign missions. In 1913 he withdrew from the diplomatic service to devote his entire time to the prosecution of his historical studies.

While acting as the representative of Brazil, Dr. Lima always interpreted his obligations with much latitude; his conception of the duties of a minister plenipotentiary differed widely from that of a conventional diplomatist. He refused to confine his talents and energies to the usual routine in which fixed conventions, meaningless etiquette and hampering restrictions play such a large part. He conceived it his mission to represent Brazil at her best or not at all. Whether in Tokyo or Brussels, in Caracas or Stockholm, he strove unceasingly to extend a wider and truer knowledge of Brazil; not only the Brazil of the present, with her astounding economic development, but also the Brazil of the past with her rich spiritual heritages, her fine traditions, her inspiring history and literature. In pursuance of this ambitious program he displayed an intellectual activity little short of prodigious. By means of lectures, articles in reviews and newspapers, books and pamphlets, he not only dispelled a host of misconceptions and prejudices; but, what was of greater moment, aroused in wide circles an eager and intelligent interest in the historical evolution and cultural development of Latin America. A brief discussion of his most significant works will clearly reveal how well he deserves the tribute of "Intellectual Ambassador of Brazil" given him by the great Swedish author Björnson.

Quite appropriately Dr. Lima's first historical production dealt with his native city. "The Historical Development of Pernambuco"[1] is a scholarly and entertaining work in which the author has traced in broad outline the social and political development of one of the most interesting cities of South America. Especially noteworthy is the account of the Dutch occupation in the sixteenth century. With the sure and deft touch of a literary artist he has drawn the portrait of the real hero of this epic adventure, the genial and tolerant Count Maurice of Nassau-Siegen, sent out by the Dutch West India Company to govern their American possessions. With the same graphic word-painting he has sketched the subsequent events which have inseparably coupled Pernambuco with the national evolution of Brazil.

In 1906 appeared a work which at once gained the author a high place among contemporary literary critics. "Some Aspects of Colonial Brazilian Literature,"[2] is a brilliant analysis of the leading tendencies of Brazilian letters in the seventeenth and eighteenth centuries. While Dr. Lima has necessarily followed in the trail blazed by that dean of literary criticism, Silvio Romero, whose "History of Brazilian Literature" has already become a classic, Dr. Lima's book reveals much originality and abounds in suggestive and in some cases new points of view. In this respect the section devoted to the school of poetry which flourished in the Captaincy of Minas Geraes during the eighteenth century should be singled out for special mention.

Dr. Lima's most valuable contribution in the purely historical field is his recent work, "Dom John VI in Brazil."[3] In this monograph all of the author's qualities as an historian appear at their best. Patient and exhaustive researches in the archives of London, Vienna, Paris and Rio de Janeiro have supplied a mass of original material out of which has been constructed a narrative of great interest and enduring value. As is well known, the period described was a critical and decisive one in the history of Brazil. The French invasion of Portugal in 1807-1808

[1] *Pernambuco, seu Desenvolvimento historico.* (Leipzig, 1895.)
[2] *Aspectos da Litteratura Colonial Brazileira.* (Leipzig, 1906.)
[3] *Dom João VI no Brazil.* 2 vols. (Rio de Janeiro, 1909.)

had caused the members of the Braganza dynasty and the Portuguese Court to take refuge in Brazil, which thus became the seat of government of the Portuguese dominions until 1821. The history of this all-important period Dr. Lima has made peculiarly his own. These thirteen years witnessed the transformation of Brazil from a stagnant colony, a mere geographical expression, into a real political unit. At the same time the Brazilian people under the fostering care of King John and his able ministers attained a degree of national self-consciousness impossible under the old colonial régime. Hence the definite separation of the colony from the mother country in 1822—"even as a ripe fruit falls from the tree"—was one of the logical results of King John's long residence in Brazil. Dr. Lima's investigations in hitherto unused sources also led to a revision of judgment of many personages and events of the period; an instance of which is his successful rehabilitation of the character of Dom John VI. This sovereign, treated with contempt and contumely by the bulk of the Portuguese historians who have never forgiven him for deserting his native land, now appears in a new and deservedly more favorable light. The author makes it clear that John's rule in Brazil was as liberal and progressive as was desirable in a country in which all thorough-going reforms must of necessity be introduced gradually. And these same reforms, especially the opening of the chief Brazilian ports to the commerce of all friendly nations, not only redounded to the immediate benefit of the country, but what was infinitely more important, paved the way for ultimate independence.

Covering as it does this wide range of important topics and written according to the most exacting canons of historical criticism, this monograph will unquestionably take its place as a standard authority.

Upon one occasion or another almost every important phase of Brazilian History has been the object of Dr. Lima's attention. The fourth centenary of the famous voyage of Cabral, brought forth an article on the discovery of Brazil.[4] Though small in compass, this study clears up a number of perplexing points and was at once recognized as a real contribution to a subject still enveloped in many obscurities. It may be noted in passing that this article was awarded the prize offered by the association under whose auspices the fourth centenary of the discovery of Brazil was celebrated. "The Recognition of the Empire, a Contribution to the Diplomatic History of Brazil,"[5] is a successful attempt to

---

[4] *Memoria sobre o descobrimento do Brasil*, premiada pela Associacão do Quatro Centenario. (Rio de Janeiro, 1900.)

[5] *O Reconhecimento do Imperio, Historia diplomatica do Brasil.* (Paris-Rio de Janeiro, 1901.)

explain the involved and tortuous diplomacy which led up to the recognition of the Empire of Brazil by Portugal and the great powers of Europe. "José Bonifacio and the Movement for Independence"[6] is a sympathetic appreciation of the character and achievements of the "Patriarch of Independence," that scholar and statesman who proved a tower of strength to the young Dom Pedro I during the stormy years when Brazil was serving her apprenticeship in self-government. "Seven Years of Republic in Brazil,"[7] an article originally published in the *Nouvelle Revue* is a remarkable synthesis of the leading events of the period 1889-1896. After analyzing the causes of the overthrow of the monarchy in 1889, the author points out that the disorders and confusion of the first years of the republic were the inevitable concomitants of the transition from an imperial to a democratic régime. Finally, mention should be made of the lectures recently given at the Sorbonne at Paris on the "Historical Formation of Brazilian Nationality."[8] This work, embodying the entire history of Brazil, is probably the most satisfactory work on the subject to be found within the compass of a single volume. Especially felicitous is the author in the last two lectures in which he points out the salient characteristics of the reign of the last emperor of Brazil, Dom Pedro "the Magnanimous." It is doubtful if a truer or more convincing appreciation has ever been written of the monarch who for nearly half a century presided over the destiny of Brazil.

A work of particular relevancy at the present time is the little volume entitled "Pan-Americanism; Bolívar-Monroe-Roosevelt." This consists primarily of a series of studies or essays dealing with the relations of the United States to Latin America. Especially suggestive are the chapters dealing with the Drago Doctrine—here set forth with unusual clearness—the evolution of the Pan-American ideal, and the Monroe Doctrine. In regard to the latter topic Dr. Lima advances the thesis, now steadily gaining in the number of its adherents, that a new basis should be found for the Monroe Doctrine. He unhesitatingly admits its value to the whole American continent "as long as it did not undergo alteration—that is to say as long as, continuing to be an arm of protection, it did not become an arm of guardianship, indeed of dominion, by means of territorial annexations." Rightly or wrongly, however, certain Latin American countries have arrived at the conviction that the Doctrine is losing its earlier, altruistic meaning and is being used as a cloak

[6] *José Bonifacio e o movimento da Independencia.* (São Paulo, 1907.)
[7] *Sept ans de République au Brésil.* (Paris, 1896.)
[8] *Formation Historique de la Nationalité Brésilienne.* (Paris, 1911.)
[9] *Pan-Americanismo, Bolívar-Monroe-Roosevelt.* (Paris-Rio de Janeiro, 1908.)

to mask the designs of their powerful neighbor to the north. If the Monroe Doctrine is to serve a beneficent purpose, if it is to promote concord rather than foment suspicions between the United States and Latin America, it must cease to be merely unilateral but must derive its sanction and effectiveness not from the United States alone but from all of America, or at least from those states whose stability and importance have won for them a definite place in the comity of nations.

The remaining works of Dr. Lima include two delightful books dealing with the author's impressions of the United States and Japan;[10] a carefully arranged bibliography of the manuscripts on Brazilian History existing in the British Museum;[11] a series of lectures on the Portuguese Language and Brazilian Literature delivered in 1909 at the University of Louvain;[12] an incisive and illuminating appreciation of the famous Brazilian novelist Machado de Assis and his works;[13] an historical drama, "The King's Secretary"—in which the eighteenth century Portuguese statesman Alexandre de Gusmão is the hero. Finally mention should be made of a work which might be called "Impressions of a Diplomat."[14] This book, embodying the results of long experience and mature study, is really a highly constructive criticism of modern diplomacy with its too great emphasis on meaningless traditions and outgrown formulæ.

Dr. Lima is a member of the Brazilian Academy, the Academy of Lisbon, and the Geographical and Historical Institute of Rio de Janeiro, in addition to a large number of other learned societies both in Europe and America. He is a member of the editing committee of the recently organized "Societé d'Histoire de l'Amérique latine" and has been entrusted with the preparation of Volume VIII of the monumental "History of Latin America" now being published by the Society. This volume, entitled "Brazil under the Imperial Régime,"[15] will unquestionably become the standard history of the Brazilian Empire.

In this brief introduction a few words regarding the general scope and character of the present volume may not be out of place. Within

---

[10] *No Japão, Impressões da terra e da gente.* (Rio de Janeiro, 1903.) *Nos Estados Unidos, Impressões politicas e sociaes.* (Leipzig, 1899.)

[11] *Relacão dos Manucriptos do Museu Britannico de interesse para o Brazil.* (Rio de Janeiro, 1903.)

[12] *La langue portugaise, La littérature brésilienne, conférences faites à l'Université de Louvain.* (Anvers, 1909.)

[13] *Machado de Assis et son oeuvre littéraire.* (Paris, 1909.)

[14] *Cousas diplomaticas.* (Lisboa, 1908.)

[15] *Le Brésil sous le régime imperial.*

the small compass of six lectures Dr. Lima has dealt with the social, political and even the intellectual evolution of Brazil, at the same time instituting comparisons with similar or parallel movements in Spanish America and in what for want of a better term may be called Anglo-Saxon America. Such an undertaking is attended with many difficulties. A merely chronological treatment would become almost inevitably an epitome of dates and proper names, a characteristic all too common to histories of Latin America. On the other hand, a series of generalizations covering the entire field would necessarily be too vague or abstract to be entirely satisfactory. Dr. Lima has frankly recognized that it would be impossible to cover adequately every phase of his subject and has therefore confined himself to a somewhat detailed discussion of a comparatively small number of topics which would presumably be of interest to an American University audience. It is obvious that this method has certain distinct advantages. It permits the lecturer, for instance, to enlarge on various problems whose solution has taxed the best energies of the inhabitants of both North and South America. Such a problem is the abolition of negro slavery. Dr. Lima is at pains to point out the different aspects which the institution of slavery assumed in Brazil, Spanish America, and the United States; he makes clear the circumstances under which abolition was accomplished; and finally explains why, in the case of Brazil, complete emancipation had to wait until nearly the end of the ninteenth century while in the case of Spanish America it synchronized with the separation of the colonies from the mother country.

Another subject capable of furnishing interesting parallels is the struggle for political independence in the various sections of the two Americas. Dr. Lima indicates certain grievances, economic, social and political, which the English, Spanish and Portuguese colonists harbored in common against their respective mother countries; grievances which in English and Spanish America culminated in the Wars of Independence. He compares at length the two great protagonists of this struggle in South America—Bolívar and San Martin; and to make the comparison still more effective he emphasizes the many points of resemblance between Bolívar and Napoleon, and San Martin and Washington. Finally, he carefully analyzes the factors which led the new nations of the two Americas to develop along divergent lines. The dignified and relatively peaceful evolution of Brazil is to be attributed in large part to the influence of an imported but thoroughly acclimated imperial dynasty, while the turbulence and anarchy so characteristic of the first decades of the Spanish American Republics find their historical explanation in certain pernicious heritages from the colonial regime, the extinction of the best elements of the population in the long and devastating Wars of Independence, and lastly unrestrained political activity divorced from civic education. That the establishment of a number of European dynasties in Spanish America would have tended towards orderly development and political cohesion is suggested by the efforts made by both San Martin and Bolívar to found in America some sort of a liberal monarchy. This important topic—the attempted foundation of a European or creole dynasty in Spanish America—receives in the present volume its first adequate treatment in English.

To pursue further this analysis of the various topics so ably discussed by Dr. Lima would not only unduly expand the limits of this brief introduction but would also infringe upon the lectures themselves. Especially suggestive, however, is the author's treatment of such subjects as the civilization of Colonial Spanish America; the relation of the colonists to the indigenous races; the role of the clergy, especially the Jesuits, during the sixteenth and seventeenth centuries; the attempt to apply the principles of federalism to communities in which the civic consciousness is rudimentary; the formative influences in the intellectual evolution of Brazil and the Spanish American Republics; and finally the growth of idealism.

In conclusion it may be noted that the topical method followed by Dr. Lima is not without its disadvantages. It is evident that only those who are in possession of a general knowledge of the leading facts of Latin American History are able fully to profit from the lecturer's generalizations and deductions. Unfortunately, owing to the fact that among us Latin America is only beginning to receive an attention commensurate with its importance, such a background of general knowledge is but rarely found even among professional students of history. To meet this situation, as well as to increase the general usefulness of the lectures, the editor has ventured to append a number of explanatory notes and bibliographical references. With few exceptions the notes refer only to events or personages connected with Latin America and the explanations are in every case as brief as is consistent with clearness. The bibliographical references are in general confined to books in English or French; Portuguese and Spanish works are cited only when more available references are lacking.

P. A. MARTIN.

STANFORD UNIVERSITY, CAL.,
    March, 1914.

LECTURE I.

The conquest of America.—Religious defence of the native element.—Indians and negroes.—The color problem and the discrimination against the colonists.—The institution of slavery and the conditions of political independence in the Spanish and Portuguese colonies, affecting diversely the abolition of slavery.—The first Spanish American civil war and the verdict of history in regard to it.—The social organization in the possessions of the New World.—The Indians and the clergy.—The part taken by the Jesuits.—The fusion of the races and the Neo-European product.—Causes of the separation: disregard of nationality and economic exploitation.—Monopolies and prohibitions.—Spiritual tutelage and emancipation.—Historical reasons for the Catholic intolerance.—Intellectual revival of the Iberian Peninsula during the Spanish reign of Charles III, and under the Portuguese dictatorship of the Marquis de Pombal.—Influence of this revival in the colonies.

THE conquest of Spanish and Portuguese America is a fairly familiar subject to the great number of those who, in the country of Prescott, cultivate the taste for reading. You have, moreover, the good fortune to count among your men of letters, historians who have given to their writings on certain foreign subjects a picturesque or romantic touch, or a documentary character, in each case superior and final. This fact deserves all the more to be noted inasmuch as it not only proves the contrary of the alleged exclusively utilitarian character of your civilization, but is moreover an evidence of your intellectuality. This is an aspect under which you are less known in our Latin-American countries, notwithstanding your university development, to which I owe my presence here today.

Thus it was by treating themes outside, so to speak, of your own evolution, and identifying themselves with these, that the name of Parkman has become inseparably associated with the history of the adventures of the French in Canada, that of Washington Irving with the Arabian life in the Vega of Andalusia and in the gardens of Granada, and that of John Lothrop Motley with the heroic struggle of the Dutch for religious freedom and the civil and political franchise. Under such circumstances it would be idle, not to say pretentious, to repeat here things you all know from the learned and charming works of your authors, and, as regards the particular subject I am about to present to you, from the works of such a distinguished historian as Prescott. I must add, however, that the study of such topics cannot but arouse a certain patriotic pride, in addition to the general human emotion called forth by such extraordinary events.

The conquest of America was, indeed, one of the decisive events both in the material and moral evolution of the world as well as in the history of mankind, and no educated person of the present day is ignorant of its social consequences; they form part of an ordinary education. The conquest of Mexico and Peru constitutes the most impressive scene of this great pageant and the most interesting feature of the achievements of the Castilians in the New World. These achievements, though attended by violence, were destined to be fruitful, since the barbarian civilizations—if we may thus designate the semi-civilizations destroyed by the European invader—represented the formless though least crude expression of the development attained by the American race, whether autochthon or immigrant. For it would be futile to deny that the Christian civilization of the Spaniards, though darkened by avarice and crime, represented a higher plane of human progress than that reached by the natives of either Mexico, Yucatan or Peru.

For this reason the great sacrifice consummated in those regions seems all the more cruel to us, the pathetic and touching figures of Guatemotzin [1] and Atahualpa [2] being special objects of our pity; but we must not forget that throughout the entire continent, from Hudson Bay to Tierra del Fuego, the struggle between the conquerors and the conquered was equally violent and bloody. Whether impelled by mere thirst for gold and silver, or urged on by less base motives, Europeans in every part of the New World employed the same system of oppression and destruction. The use of such methods seems to us perhaps greater among the Spanish than among the English and Portuguese, not because they really were so, but because our imagination demands that the methods of conquest should be in proportion to the results obtained. Yet, notwithstanding the great wealth of gold and diamonds existing in the Brazilian plateau of Minas Geraes [3] during the eighteenth century, no other metropolis having trans-Atlantic colonies could have boasted, as did the Spanish, that from the gold and silver mines of Mexico alone it had received during the colonial period, as the *quinto* or fifth due the royal treasury, more than ten thousand millions of dollars.

It is therefore not surprising that Spain should have wasted all her energies in the maintenance of an empire across the seas which was the real source of her wealth. Yet a closer scrutiny would show that this wealth was more apparent than real. During the course of the sixteenth and seventeenth centuries Spain had changed from a producing to an intermediary nation, from a manufacturing to a trading nation. The causes of this momentous transformation are familiar to all students of Spanish History. They were on the one hand the depopulation of the country due to the expulsion of the Moors and Jews, colonial adventures, European wars, and the fires of the Inquisition; and on the other hand, the exhaustion, if not the complete extinction, of many of her long established industries through the elimination of the skilled Arab element. When these circumstances are taken into account, it need occasion no surprise that the greater part of the wealth obtained from America was diverted to other centers more given over to professional pursuits than to the glory of conquest.

This lust for conquest, however, made a peculiar appeal to the popular fancy of a people of Celtic characteristics, and to the fighting instincts of a nation possessing warlike traditions. If you will read the translation of that true and stirring novel called the "Narrative of the Cortez Expedition," by Bernal Diaz del Castillo [4], a translation written in flawless French by José Maria de Heredia [5] the Academician and talented author of *Les Trophées*—you will see the enthusiasm with which, during the first half of the sixteenth century, expeditions of this kind were organized in Spain, and you will be able to appreciate the appeal they made to the imagination of nobles and plebeians alike, and the animal fury with which all threw themselves into the storming and plundering of those unknown and fabulous treasures. Would it be possible to impress ideas of moderation and kindness upon a people in such an excited and frenzied state of mind, when the lowest motives and passions dominated and overpowered all the higher instincts?

If the Portuguese did not evince equal enthusiasm for Brazil, which was the portion destiny had allotted them in the distribution of the newly discovered lands, it was because the marvels of India were at that time engrossing all their attention. It is altogether probable that had the Spanish controlled the Hindustan peninsula, they would not have held so fast from the very beginning to the islands and mainland from which they began their difficult conquest of the New World. It is only in fable that the dog is seen to let go his prey and run after its shadow. The Hindu civilization, before it produced its deleterious effects, like the legendary shade of the *manchineel* tree [6] dazzled the invaders and awoke in them delightful dreams of lustful pleasures easily gratified.

History, in its description of deeds of bloodshed and violence, is, in its entirety, but a sad and monotonous story. It is not so very long ago that peace became for a great many a noble ideal: in the country of

Brutus and Cato, as in that of the Cid and the Duke of Alva, it would have been regarded as a sign of cowardice, a thing to be ashamed of. In Spanish and Portuguese America, however, there is seen from the very beginning a movement of compassion for and protection of the native element, tyrannized and reduced to slavery by the fury of the invaders. This fact is greatly to the credit of the respective mother countries, and does especial honor to their religious orders, for, despite the fact that they regarded the oppressed race as inferior, they did not judge it to be devoid of moral sense and without soul.

The name of Las Casas [7], whose work was confined chiefly to the Antilles, since they constituted the field of Spain's first adventures and territorial occupations, is one that is justly popular among you; but perhaps you may not know that the name of Anchieta [8], one of the Jesuits who devoted themselves heart and soul to the catechization of the Indians, was no less worthy of veneration. Both in the conversion of the Indians, and in their ministry to the spiritual needs of the colonists, intent on the gratification of their appetites, the priests of the Jesuit Order rendered such remarkable services in Brazil that it is no exaggeration to say that they were the principal agents of our national culture, particularly during the sixteenth and seventeenth centuries, that is, during the period in which the new society was adapting itself to its new surroundings.

You may say that the intervention of the clergy in behalf of the Indians was after all of little practical value. The government of the mother country was too far away to supervise the strict enforcement of the decrees which, from feelings of justice or mercy, had been extorted from its representatives.¹ Moreover, the local conditions of gross sensuality and greed, such as they first appear to us, were ill calculated to foster feelings of compassion. Spanish American writers even say that the caste known as the creole, that is the white American-born descendants of the conquerors and colonists who formed the local nobility, was distinguished by pride based chiefly on the purity of the white race.

This purity of race was not in a certain way as much prized in Portuguese America as in the Viceroyalty of Buenos Aires or even in the Viceroyalties of Lima, Bogotá and Mexico, where intermarriage with the Indian was far more common than with the negro. But this mixture of

¹ In speaking of the government of the mother country I refer especially to the power of the king, who was in all respects above the tribunals and councils which exercised jurisdiction over the colonies. Of these bodies, the former were traditional institutions of Portugal, while the latter, of Spanish origin, were established during the union of the Iberian kingdoms (1580-1640).

blood did not lessen the inhumanities practised, nor cause pity to blossom in the human heart. It is well known that no slaves were more unfortunate than those belonging to the colored slave-owners, where these were allowed to possess them, and that the overseers, whose cruelty to the slaves is proverbial, were chosen from among the freed slaves or those of mixed blood rather than from the European or immigrant element.

The numerical predominance of those of mixed Indian blood over those of mixed negro blood in the greater part of Spanish America, is the natural result of the conditions prevailing in those countries. In comparing these with the conditions existing in Brazil, it is necessary to keep in mind that the Indian population of that part of the American territory occupied by the Spaniards was denser and in part more amenable to discipline than that of the territory occupied by the Portugese, and therefore offered greater facilities for the recruiting by force of colonial laborers. It must be further recognized that up to the time of the Treaty of Utrecht (1713), the African slave trade, which could have supplied such laborers, never ceased to be a monopoly of the government, like any other branch of the colonial trade, the respective licenses or concessions being sold at a very high price, a circumstance which enhanced the cost of negro labor, and at the same time stimulated the contraband trade.

It was, as you know, at the Congress of Utrecht that Spain was obliged to abandon her system of commercial monopoly, permitting France to trade with Peru and Chile by way of Cape Horn, and through the famous *Asiento* treaty ceding to England for thirty years the privilege of the African slave trade with the Spanish possessions, at the same time permitting her to establish factories at certain points in Spanish America.

I touched a few moments ago on the ever burning question of race feeling. It is a sentiment which among you has reached a degree of intensity which has never been equalled among the Americans of Iberian descent, although these too show in small degree a contempt for all persons of color. Indeed, not only has the genealogical tree of many families of distinction been jealously guarded from contact with all strains of inferior blood, but the whites of the colonies maintained and defended their titles and rights to certain posts and functions, which had been reserved to them by the laws of their respective mother countries.

Nor were reasons wanting for this racial antagonism, for already a son of the colony, or creole, was placed for this very reason in a position of marked inferiority in the public life of the time. The best posts were in fact, though not by law, unjustly reserved for the sons of the mother country, as individual rewards for the collective effort of conquest. To be sure the colonists succeeded eventually in securing many of the judicial and government offices, but what would have become of the white creoles if the negroes and the mulattoes could have competed with them or had been placed on a parity in the distribution of the official posts and honors?

It is known that the Indians were not victims of the full application of this discrimination, some of them even having been admitted to the nobility; but the army, which is the symbol of effective dominion, never failed to be European in its command, if not in its rank and file, the mulattoes among the local militia forming its private regiments in which they could rise to the post of captain. A parallel for such a situation might be found at the present time in the conditions existing in Hindustan.

No person of mixed or Indian blood was allowed to matriculate in the University of San Marcos in Lima or enroll in the embryonic Faculty of Medicine of Los Reyes, that is to say, in the two institutions of higher learning in the opulent capital of Peru. The wealth and culture of colonial Lima may be gaged from the fact that in the eighteenth century no less than four thousand carriages were to be seen on its streets,[2] while this same capital was such a spirited intellectual center that the contests for the professorships in the University produced genuine disturbances, giving rise to factions which did not hesitate to come to blows.

If a *mestizo* of very light color succeeded in gaining entrance to these institutions of higher learning it was because of the difficulty in proving that he was not of pure blood. One of the viceroys, Count of Monclova [9], went so far as to decree that in such cases, once the mixed blood had been proved, the degree given should be cancelled. The order must have given rise to protests and appeals to the Supreme Council of the Indies, for royal decisions confirmed it in 1752, and later in 1758, banishing from the liberal professions all colonial subjects who were not direct descendants of Spaniards. These same decrees, however, excepted those who, in 1697, had been declared free from mixed blood, of noble birth and qualified for the exercise of high offices, that is to say, the Indian *caciques* [10] and their offspring.

The Church was more liberal than the State, for it not only admitted into its association all new converts, but occasionally raised them to the priesthood, without making any distinction between the subject Indians and their chiefs. It is significant, however, that the Indians took but little advantage of these favors. In the mother countries scruples of blood were less strong, for there the same conditions of competition did

---

[2] Burck: *Histoire des Colonies européennes dans l'Amérique.*

not prevail, and consequently this color problem, which miscegenation was silently solving, seemed less acute and less irritating than in the colonies.

In the beginning of the eighteenth century, the government of Spain, driven by the needs of its treasury, went so far as to sell certificates of white blood—the famous *cedulas de gracias al sacar*—the cost of which naturally increased in proportion to the doubtfulness of the color of the aspirant to a certificate of pure blood. Justification for such liberalism was found in the Christian religion, which anticipating political revolutions had made all men equal. It is to be noted, however, that those who advanced such a pretext for social philanthropy neglected to mention the fact that the Catholic Church had forgotten to condemn negro slavery while that nefarious traffic was still in its infancy.

The missionaries, absorbed as they were in the work of freeing the natives, the immediate victims of slavery and destruction, and at the same time realizing that some one was needed to work for the white man under tropical skies and in a territory that was but sparsely settled, looked indulgently, or at least without protest, upon the importation of African negroes. In Brazil, the first cry for abolition was in reality made by a priest, who wrote the *Ethiope Resgatado* (The Ethiopian Redeemed) [11], but this was not until the middle of the eighteenth century.

Meanwhile the Indians in Brazil benefited from a continuous protective legislation which was strengthened by the Jesuits in proportion as the existing laws were disregarded by the colonists, and they found themselves at last in the full enjoyment of their rights under the ministry of the Marquis of Pombal [12], precisely in the middle of the eighteenth century, when the lot of the negro was beginning to awaken public interest.

The circumstance under which the independence of Spanish America was effected permitted or rather determined the abolition of slavery in many of the former colonies. In the case of Brazil, however, the economic importance of slavery was so much greater than in Spanish America that the slave trade continued even after 1851, the year of its official extinction, and the institution of slavery as such only ended in our own time, in 1888, and then without any social upheaval, but rather in an atmosphere of liberal concord. That which in Brazil was the result of gradual evolution, effected under normal conditions, so to speak, was in most of Spanish America hurried on by an acute crisis in the midst of a process of transformation.

The attitude on the part of the land-holding classes during the period in which Latin America achieved her political independence explains, in part at least, the prompt abolition of slavery in the greater part of the former Spanish colonies and its retention for nearly a century longer in Brazil. In Spanish America the slave owners were largely to be found among the inhabitants of European descent, the mine owners and planters, in fine, those who through self-interest or political loyalty—a loyalty strengthened by a bloody and terrible war—remained faithful to the mother country. Under the circumstances the success of the Spanish American Revolutions, in which these royalists went down to defeat, was logically accompanied by the official extinction of slavery. In Portuguese America, on the other hand, where the political separation from the mother country was accompanied by little armed strife, the problem of slavery did not become so acute. The land-holding class in the main identified itself with the new régime and was consequently left in undisturbed possession of its slaves. To be sure we had in a later epoch such episodes as the so-called *cabanadas* or guerillas, which between 1832 and 1835 devastated Pernambuco, but these guerilla bands, so called "Partisans of absolutism," were much more armed agents of pillage and plunder than the representatives of an older political faith.

Did time permit, it would be interesting to point out certain analogies between the problem of slavery in the United States—a problem whose solution was due to Lincoln—and the problem as it existed in Brazil. I may only state in passing that although abolition was certainly the realization of a beautiful humanitarian ideal, its sudden victory in your country was due to the struggle caused by the resistance of the partisans of slavery. The Union would not have decreed the freedom, immediate, complete, and without compensation, of the slave element, if the union of the nation had not been in imminent jeopardy and if the cause of slavery had not given rise to a bloody conflict. An act of humanity, it is true, but an act of retaliation also, which does not, however, annul its moral grandeur, nor destroy its beneficent results.

In Brazil, the reconciliation between the Portuguese and Brazilians which followed shortly after the bloodless separation from the mother country permitted the prompt establishment of an economic *modus vivendi*, whereby slave labor was retained until the moral and political evolution of the country demanded its abolition by legislative enactment.

This harmony between the two discordant elements, under the ever peaceful influence of the monarchy, resulted in a comparative absence of internal dissensions and in the complete allayment of the revolutionary animosities, after a short period of adaptation to the new régime. The

Wars of Independence in Spanish America, on the other hand, created a restlessness which had become proverbial, and traces of which still linger even in those countries which have definitely entered upon a period of peace and national progress.

Indeed, the Spanish-American War of Independence may be regarded, as the distinguished Venezuelan scholars Laureano Vallanilla-Lanz and Angel Cesar Rivas recently declared in public lectures given at Caracas, as the first of the internal political struggles of the disrupted colonial empire. The contest was of a civil, far more than of an international, character, in sharp contrast to your War of Independence, in which individual rights and self-government served as a pretext for a duel across the seas between England and France, which had for its object and reward, preeminence on the seas, together with colonial supremacy.

In a civil war, one of the belligerent parties either assumes the attributes of the sovereign state and identifies itself with it or is swallowed up in the vortex of the struggle. Spanish America gained its sovereignty, but from a certain point of view the struggle had pernicious effects which time alone will correct. It is here that the genesis of its revolutions is to be found, just as the Roman conquest is contained in embryo in the first fables of its history:—the killing of Remus by his brother Romulus, and the rape of the Sabines. The Colombian author, Carlos Holguin, accurately describes the situation when he says that "from that time it became an established principle with this people that war was as legitimate a means as any other for obtaining personal advantage, and one by which the desperate could make use of rich probabilities of their becoming masters of their fellow-citizens; the sacred right to insurrection constituted the foundation of the Republic and the fountain head of all other rights."

You all know that the verdicts of history, or the manner of judging historical events, frequently undergo modification. The feelings and prejudices of the time, both individual and collective, naturally influence the manner of regarding events of the past, giving rise to different and even contradictory estimates at different periods, and even in the same period. To cite a striking instance, the French revolution which at first was generally regarded as a salvation, was afterwards declared to be an infamous and useless spilling of blood, only to be again deified, then villified, and finally considered on the whole as a redemption, although a nightmare and a disgrace in some of its features.

Historical criticism is passing through a somewhat similar evolution in the case of the Spanish American War of Independence. Its aspect as a struggle for political emancipation has been examined into by minds less given to enthusiasm and more diligent in the search for facts. These scholars, while not denying its heroic texture, have, nevertheless, found that in many of the engagements of this cruel war, the struggle was less between the Spanish forces and the revolutionary patriots, than between subjects of the same color, in behalf of interests and passions which were then disguised under the name of the "Prisoner King" [13], just as later the same interests and passions were veiled with other more abstract names.

Bolívar was, moreover, the first to recognize the fact. In one of his stirring proclamations, issued as he was abandoning in defeat the field of action to which he was later to return more energetic than ever, we read the following words addressed to his compatriots: "Your brothers and not the Spaniards have torn your breasts, spilled your blood, set fire to your homes and driven you from your country. Your cries should be turned against these blind slaves who seek to bind you to their own chains of slavery. A few successes on the part of our adversaries have ruined the edifice of our glory, the mass of the people being misled by religious fanaticism and seduced by anarchy."

You in the United States were much more fortunate, for those whom Laboulaye [14], in treating of this subject, calls domestic enemies, were rare. In Latin America, Chile alone, on account of the peculiar conditions of its settlement, which was effected by a hard-fought struggle between the colonists and the natives—the fearful Araucanians [15]—was accustomed to well defined parties and at the moment of separation showed uniformity in each of the contending factions. Thus it succeeded in preserving its social organization, which continued to strengthen itself in the separation of the classes and in the ascendency of those of the upper stratum, forming a close oligarchy of whites. The democratic spirit is already opening a breach in this construction, which from its very nature is incapable of withstanding the destructive action of time. Such a peculiar social structure secured, however, to the country a century of assured material progress and an administrative stability superior to any other in Spanish America. Hence it may be said to represent an epoch of national development, just as the Gothic cathedrals represent the period of the most ardent Catholic faith.

In Venezuela, the war-school *par excellence* of this cycle of independence, there happened what is thus described by Sr. Vallanilla-Lanz, in periods as eloquent and sonorous as are to be found in all Spanish

American literature: "The flower of our society succumbed beneath the sword of barbarism, and of the great and noble class which produced Simon Bolívar, there remained, after Carabobo [16] (the battle which decided the fate of the colony), only a few living skeletons that wandered here and there over the Antilles, and other dead ones that marked this broad path of glory extending from Ávila to Potosí" [17]. The whites had indeed gradually disappeared amid the misfortunes of the campaign, and in many towns of the country only men of color were left to represent the triumphant democracy. The old colonial hierarchy had been swallowed up in the revolutionary maëlstrom.

The colonial society may be said to have been regularly constituted at the time when the Indians were granted a civil status and the ransom of the slaves was first advocated. At the top were the high European officials subject to the Viceroy or Captain-General; immediately below were the colonial whites of noble birth, almost all of whom were planters; below these and competing with them were the merchants from the mother country who had come to enrich themselves in the transatlantic provinces; and finally, at the bottom, were the various strata of the common people, very much intermingled—the freemen of mixed blood, Indians apparently free, negro and mulatto slaves.

In the sum of transactions which this society in a stable state represented, was that of religion itself, for, thanks to the self-interest of its minister, religion conformed, practically at least, if not theoretically, to the methods so vigorously denounced in the early days of colonization. Antonio de Ulloa and Jorge Juan [18], the distinguished Spanish scientists who came to America in the wake of La Condamine [19] and the French Mission to measure the terrestrial degree at the equator, describe in their *Noticias Secretas de America* (Secret Notices of America), which were not published until after the independence of the Spanish possessions, how the regular curates exploited the Indians like any *encomendero*.

You are undoubtedly acquainted with this expression which is familiar in American history and which signifies the holder of a royal favor or grant, by which a certain extension of land was given to him, together with the Indians inhabiting it, on condition that the concessionaire or holder of the trust should protect, convert and instruct them. As this trust of souls was not undertaken without a certain amount of obligatory personal labor on the part of the other party, it is easy to calculate, if we recall the *milieu,* the abuses to which such a system would give rise, and although various attempts were made to eliminate the most objectionable features, it was not finally abolished until the time of Charles III, a monarch whose reforms deserve to be known and admired [20].

The assertion of Ulloa and Juan needs no corroboration, for their trustworthiness is well known; however, it will not be amiss to give in this connection the opinion of the Frenchman Depons [21], who, in 1806, four years before the outbreak of the revolution, wrote a book on Venezuela which is still very highly esteemed. According to him the priests arrived from Spain with good intentions, but finding their associates given up to a life which conformed far more to the spirit of man than to the spirit of God, human frailty found it much easier to follow their example than to set a different one.

This witty remark explains why the laws drawn up in Spain and Portugal by the councils which superintended the colonial administration—the Council of the Indies in Spain, and the Council of the Colonies in Portugal—and ordered by the monarchs who were under the spiritual sway of the Jesuits, remained a dead letter on the other side of the ocean, especially when the first fever of evangelization had passed. As a result, the social elevation of the American Indians was a complete failure. The brilliant Venezuelan writer, Blanco Fombona [22], in recent lectures given at Madrid, observes, and rightly, that Juarez and Altamirano [24], both Mexicans, were the only men of eminence which the red race produced in the nineteenth century.

You will recall that in Juarez were incarnated the two principles which played an all important part in the historical evolution of the Mexican nation. The first was the spirit of national resistance to the attempt to establish a monarchy which had the grave defect of appearing as the defender of threatened political elements, and the still graver one of availing itself of foreign aid and personating itself in a foreign dynasty; the second, which was still more noteworthy, was the principle of secular or anti-clerical government, with which the institution of democracy was identified in that country.

I used the word Jesuit for the second time a few moments ago, and without any defamatory intention, in referring to the influence which this order so long enjoyed in the confessionals of the court and in the royal cabinets. The recollection may cause fear and trembling to the free-thinker of the type of the apothecary *Homais* [25], whom those of you who are familiar with French Literature will remember to have seen so admirably sketched by Gustave Flaubert in *Madame Bovary;* or to the *Carbonario* regicide [26] who, in the confines of western Europe, in the seat of our ancient and glorious metropolis, has endeavored to discredit the republican regime. Such recollection, however, has no terrors for the impartial student of historical events, who knows that in North, as well as in South America, the memory of the Jesuit cannot fail to evoke feelings of emotion and gratitude.

I think it is unnecessary for me to emphasize, as far as you are concerned, the part which Father Marquette played in the exploration of your Great West, for his statue in the Capitol at Washington, louder than any words of mine, will speak for all time. Among us, that is, in Portuguese America, the Jesuits exerted a greater social influence than in Spanish America, where, owing to the circumstances under which the discovery was made—for you all know the effect on the destiny of Columbus, of his residence in the monastery of La Rabida—other more powerful religious orders preceded them and were better able to offset the preponderance of the famous Order of Jesus and compete successfully in the steeplechase for the conversion of the savage and the education of youth.

The monks in Spain and their dependencies did not permit the Jesuits, in spite of the untiring activity of the sons of St. Ignatius of Loyola, to enjoy more than a relative half-light. In Brazil, on the contrary, all the dramatic color of the sixteenth, seventeenth, and eighteenth centuries is furnished by the conflicts between the Jesuit missionaries and the *bandeirantes*, that is, the gold seekers and slave hunters. The missionaries were found to be in the interior, some trying to protect, others to reduce to slavery the Indian tribes which, after the first hostilities and disasters, had gradually deserted the coast.

These cruel and bloody conflicts might have inflamed race hatreds had it not been for the gradual disappearance of racial prejudice through the combined influence of intermarriage and miscegenation. The result of this intermingling of the races was a multitude of mulattoes who, through a process of evolution and selection, are being formed into a new variety of the white race in which the old European element predominates. Other important factors in this racial transformation have been the decrease in the aboriginal population, the cessation of negro importation, and the constant and considerable increase in European immigration.

At the recent Congress of Races, which was held at London in July, 1911,[3] the Brazilian delegate, J. B. de Lacerda, a distinguished anthro-

---

[3] This Congress accomplished the miracle of discussing peacefully and calmly one of the questions which most divides humanity today, with such broadmindedness that the United States was officially represented by a colored physician.

pologist and Director of the National Museum of Rio de Janeiro, and a white man, presented a paper on the Brazilian mulattoes in which he gave a series of conclusions, of which I shall mention two, which agree fully with what I have just pointed out to you. One is that the mulatto, the product of the union of the white with the negro, does not truly form a race, but an ethnical type, variable, transitory and having a tendency to return to one of the races, the original factors of this union. This natural tendency of the mulatto, writes the author, is seen most clearly in those transformations which populations of mixed blood in time undergo, when marriages obey no fixed social rules and mulattoes are allowed to unite freely with whites, begetting offspring which more nearly approaches the white than the black race.

His other conclusion is that the constant increase in the number of white immigrants, sexual selection, and the disappearance of race prejudice, are coöperating towards the extinction within a short time, of the mulattoes in Brazil, a country which will become in the future, and, according to all indications, in the not far distant future, a nursery of the white race and a center of Latin civilization [27].

The same reflection applies to the Spanish American world, having due regard to its proportions. If throughout Latin America, from a strictly social standpoint, the creole or American-born white, notwithstanding the continual process of racial fusion, considered himself entirely distinct and much superior to the colored population which was in part descended from him, the native-born Spaniard or Portuguese, in his turn, considered himself superior to the creole, whether he was—to use an adaptation of the French *déraciné*—an uprooted government employee, priest, or clerk.

This lack of consideration for the creole population of the colonies, even though of noble birth and of liberal education, came to be, moreover, one of the most powerful incentives of the independence movement, when the clock of time struck the inevitable hour for the political separation of the mother country from her possessions which had more or less reached adult age. Your example, however, is proof that this kind of puberty is not more precocious under tropical skies.

This inferior status of the creole in comparison with native born Spaniards or Portuguese was by no means the only grievance of the colonists. An equally important factor in the movement towards political emancipation was the discontent resulting from the economic exploitation by a system of exclusiveness and privilege characteristic of European colonial policy until comparatively recent times. Both causes were slow to develop. You ought all the more to understand this, since they were essentially the same causes which gave rise to your glorious independence. There was the same resistance to paying taxes which they had not voted, and the same righteous indignation at not being included among those who could establish such taxes, when they possessed the same titles and qualifications. But in the Spanish and Portuguese colonies the abuses in this respect went still further. Thus to take an example at random, early in the eighteenth century, Venezuela was delivered into the hands of a company known as the Guipuzcoa Company [28]. As a result of the monarch's many favors which stopped short only at the cession of sovereignty, this company was able to govern Venezuela in all commercial matters at its discretion, and, as may be guessed, entirely in its own interest. Commercial companies organized after the manner of the Dutch trading companies of the seventeenth century, flourished in Brazil, especially in Para and Maranhão, whose unexplored resources it was proposed to develop by making such a seductive appeal to private capital.

It was with this idea in mind that the great Jesuit Antonio Vieira [29], one of the most distinguished writers of the Portuguese language and a man of subtle and keen mentality, proposed in the middle of the seventeenth century exemption from confiscation of all property belonging to these companies, whether merchandise or money. The primary object of this proposal was the attraction of Jewish capital, hitherto suspicious of the prevailing religious intolerance. Unfortunately this enlightened plan of Father Vieira was never carried out owing to the opposition of the Inquisition.

The companies, which were organized later in the middle of the eighteenth century by the Marquis of Pombal, of which the most important, the Pará-Maranhão Company [30], rendered valuable aid in the development and exploitation of a hitherto much neglected region, had beside their main object, which was economic, the political object of freeing the country from the financial tutelage of the English whom the Portugese nation had been serving simply as intermediary, providing herself with their industrial products and sending thither her gold. But the processes followed by the new companies could not be made to vary from the usual ones, which consisted in selling European goods high and buying colonial products cheap.

It was this same method which was followed by the merchants of Seville, who made Terra Firma and Panamá centers for the distribution of their cargoes, and pocketed the profits from their exports to the West Indies, a traffic which was reserved exclusively to the subjects of Castile, and which the industrious Catalans only began to enjoy legally in 1765 and 1775, or towards the end of the colonial period.

To summarize—and I am doing nothing more than pointing out a few facts among a hundred which might be cited in giving even a condensed statement of Spain's and Portugal's jealous commercial and industrial policy in the colonies,—a policy which I am not censuring, for it corresponds to the ideas which were dominant in this period and which are still powerful at the present time—factories were forbidden in Brazil, as well as in Spanish America, the production of various articles was stopped, the cultivation of the vine and the olive was made illegal in order to prevent the products of the colonies from entering into competition with the wine and oil of the mother country, and in Brazil even printing offices were prohibited. For instance a printing office, which was opened at Rio de Janeiro in the middle of the eighteenth century, was ordered closed as soon as the offence became known in Lisbon.

In this respect Spain was more liberal, for not only did the printing press accompany the government in its colonial establishment,—the first printing press of America having been established in Mexico in 1538, for Philadelphia did not have one until 1686,—but universities were created in Mexico and in Peru in the middle of the sixteenth century. In compensation for this relative, though important intellectual advantage, the Spanish American possessions, in their economic inter-relations, were subjected to even more stringent regulations than those which in Brazil constituted an obstacle to national unity. You will appreciate the situation to which I refer if you will recall the difficulties experienced by the founders of your constitution in putting an end to those trade barriers between the states of the Federation, which prevented the formation of a common consciousness necessary to their joint evolution.

I do not wish to exaggerate the liberality or rather liberalism of the Spanish Government. Its colonial universities seemed to the metropolis to be safeguarded against intellectual innovations, since their spiritual direction was confided to religious congregations interested in preserving mental immobility. If in these schools of higher learning the theological spirit ruled officially in all its obduracy, it was because the same spirit prevailed in the schools of the mother country. Neither would it be reasonable to expect that the colonies should so far have outstripped the mother country in the matter of positive progress as to oppose the deliberate darkness in which the shining light of the Renaissance had been extinguished in the Iberian Peninsula.

Besides, every society has the right to defend itself and is accustomed to exercise this right freely. Thus it is not surprising that Catholic Europe—and when we speak of Catholic Europe, we immediately and involuntarily think of the Iberian countries where the Catholic fervor was most pronounced—endeavored to guard its religious unity in the sixteenth century against two equally powerful enemies; one the infidel, the Mussulman, who, having been expelled from Spain at the close of the fifteenth century, had not only taken possession of Constantinople, the creation of the first Christian emperor of the East, but was also destined, at the end of the seventeenth century, in spite of Lepanto and the heroism of the Slavs in the Balkans, to advance triumphant until he should encamp beneath the walls of Vienna; the other was the Protestant dissenter, who, for the sake of his faith, was sowing discord throughout Europe, dragging entire countries to the side of the Reformation, and digging a wide trench which was being simultaneously filled with the blood of people of the same Christian faith, divided into partisans and enemies of Rome.

The spirit of intolerance which arose from this reaction against a threatening and imminent peril was the cause of the comparative intellectual isolation, which from that time forward, or at least for a certain period, characterized the people over whom the authority of the traditional Church was maintained intact. In conjunction with the mother country's system of government tutelage already mentioned this spirit of intolerance undoubtedly exerted a pernicious influence on the Spanish and Portuguese colonies in America.

If, indeed, the ecclesiastical censorship was active and persistent, the civil censorship was no less so. The two were allied in certain matters, as, for example, in the laws relating to printing, which prescribed that the consent of the Council of the Indies, at Madrid, was necessary for the publication, even in the colonies, of all works relating to the colonial possessions.[4] This prohibition included both Spain and Spanish America and, together with the special censorship which applied to all printed matter not included under the head of books of devotion, works on the Indian languages, on colonial jurisprudence or panegyrics of courtiers, sufficiently explains the kind of literary production which was turned out by the local printing presses.

These works afforded ample vent, however, for the intellectual proclivities of the new world. A learned paper on this subject, by Don Vicente G. Quesada, the distinguished president of the Faculty of Philos-

[4] Law of September 21, 1560.

ophy and Letters of the University of Buenos Aires, was presented at the next to the last Congress of Americanists then meeting for the first time in Latin America [31]. It is true that nearly all volumes published in colonial Spanish America deserve to be sent to the literary graveyards to which the distinguished Lord Rosebery has sarcastically alluded, and yet, notwithstanding the fact that freedom of thought was unknown at that period—and indeed it is not a universal conquest even at the present time—the press exercised in Spanish America as elsewhere, its quickening influence.

Notwithstanding these prohibitions of the official censor—and among the prohibited books were included not only the *Encyclopédie*, which, it was feared, might revolutionize the minds of the people, but also books on colonial subjects printed in Spain and abroad that had not been previously reviewed by the Council of the Indies—the philosophic doctrines of the eighteenth century succeeded in penetrating into the forbidden territory by means of contraband books and there effecting the mental transformation which was to result in the independence of Latin America. It is enough for me to mention that, in 1794, a considerable time before the war between the mother country and her colonies had broken out, the *Rights of Man* was translated and clandestinely published at Bogotá [32].

Evidences of the depth and influence of this intellectual ferment were already being forced upon the mother country in no uncertain manner. There were already unmistakable warnings of the separation when the more daring of the colonists, seizing the propitious moment, would raise their voices in favor of divorce. Once more it was shown that it is not in vain that the world moves forward, and that contact with any point on the surface of a homogeneous body tends to spread to the entire mass, the better the conductor of the vibration, the better the transmission. The epoch of the reign of Charles III, which extended from 1759 to 1788, or up to the year preceding that of the taking of the Bastile, was also for the countries south of the Pyrenees a period of intellectual transformation, the general policy and events of which have not as yet been sufficiently studied, since the profound transformation through which Spain passed in the eighteenth century, under the influence of the general renewal of ideas in the cultivated world, and especially in Western Europe, extended to the colonies, although, owing to the great distance traversed, the impulse was naturally less strongly felt there.

How otherwise is to be explained the fact that in 1779, when the mother country was in the enjoyment of full and undisputed supremacy, a man across the sea was found boldly attacking the methods of university instruction then in force? How is it possible to understand this personality, if the *milieu* was completely hostile to such ideas and there was such absolute ignorance that criticism passed for a case of mental teratology? I refer to Dr. Espejo, the author of the satire *O Novo Luciano* or *O Despertar dos Espiritos* (The New Lucian or The Awakening of Minds), an able surgeon, a man of encyclopaedic mind, and a sarcastic writer. His views were declared by the President of Quito to be seditious and odious and caused him to be rigorously dealt with by the public powers; but during his exile from Bogotá, the reformer established a school for the propagation of his ideas, and counted among his pupils the ardent Nariño [33], who was the owner of a library of revolutionary books, the translator of the *Rights of Man*, already referred to, and the center of the youthful hopes of his country, before he became the adventurous and persecuted missionary of liberal aspirations.

In the Spanish metropolis the revolution may be said to have started from the top, just as it did in the Portuguese metropolis, where the Marquis de Pombal, while strengthening the absolute system, gave free course to the new ideas in the economic, as well as in the educational domain, and in expelling the *Company of Jesus*, dealt a decisive blow to the power of the Church and to ecclesiastical prestige [34].

After the expulsion of the Jesuits, which, as you know, took place in Portugal, Spain, and France, the government of Charles III decreed that the confiscated property of this order, instead of passing to the royal domain, should be administered by a Junta, or council called *Junta de Temporalidades*, and employed in establishing schools and charitable institutions. The occasion was opportune, therefore, for substituting more modern methods—methods more in harmony with general conditions of western culture—for the old methods with which religious instruction in the Peninsula and the colonies had been identified.

Various, indeed, are the reports and opinions which government officials and commissioners published at this time, protesting against the general backwardness of the colonial mind, which, it must not be forgotten, reflected that of the mother country. In these reports they advocated the official reform of the course of studies, such as was already beginning to be done privately, as is testified by the number and worth of the emancipated minds whose work was so fruitful that its influence has reached down to the present time.

"The century was closing," writes Don Vicente Quesada, "with all the colonies feeling a certain instinctive restlessness, the precursor of the new life; ideas were taking a new flight, and the creoles, the children of the land, those who were really interested in the progress of the country, were beginning to secure the means necessary to provide for their needs; the former pupils were finding out that they no longer needed their tutors of the Peninsula, nor was it necessary to ask permission, either to express their thoughts, or to promote their well being."

So, Latin American independence was as logical a result as was your independence, and was produced by an identical state of mind, differing in degree but not in essence.

LECTURE II

European ideas brought over the sea by contraband books and native travelers.—Intercourse between mother country and colony.—The intellectual progress of the New World of Latin America before its political emancipation.—Comparison with the progress of the British possessions.—The race, environment, and period.—The race problem in America.—Traditional sympathy felt in Latin America for the inferior races.—State of the colonial culture in the Iberian and Anglo-Saxon sections.—Territorial conquest of Portuguese and Spaniards.—The political unit: the municipal chambers and *cabildos*.—Their conception and realization in the colonies and their significance in the mother countries of Europe.—The *Cabildo* of Montevideo and the part it took in the Revolution.—The municipal chambers of Brazil and Independence.—The politcial and social reconstruction of the new countries.—Education and charity.—Characteristics of colonial education.—The lack of political education in Latin Ameria.—The general characteristics of particularism and the American conception of federalism.

WE mentioned the other day, as a symptom of conditions, the rise and growth in the plateau of Cundinamarca [1], of the principles underlying the French Revolution. Here, where a hundred years before there had wandered only Indians, unprotected from the cold and ignorant of all rights of the individual with respect to the community, there was now to be found a society of European character which was secretly but ardently reading the political and social writings brought from the other side of the ocean. These ideas of reform were also propagated by the sons of the colonies who, in appreciable though incomparably smaller number than is the case today, came to Europe to travel and soon became familiar with the dominant ideas and aspirations in the lands of culture, a term which in the present case signifies France and England.

Do not think that at any time there did not exist any personal intercourse between the colonial subjects of the Iberian Peninsula and these more progressive countries. We, too, had our Franklins of a certain kind. The Brazilian epic poet, Basilio da Gama [2], in the poem "O Uruguay" has immortalized the resistance made by the natives of the Missions of Uruguay to the transfer of sovereignty over this territory from Spain to Portugal. Though born in the interior province of Minas Geraes, that land of gold and diamonds, he went to Rome and became a member of the arcadia. Alexandre de Gusmão [3], of Santos, in the

State of São Paulo, polished and refined at Paris a mind that was naturally Parisian, and hence his acuteness of vision to discern the absurdities in the court of Dom John V [4], of whom he was both private secretary as well as annalist, for his letters form the best criticism of his reign.

Moreover the intellectual men of Portugal in the eighteenth century seem to us to be in no small part Brazilians; that is to say, the number of Brazilians who, for the want of institutions of higher learning in their own land, came to Coimbra [5] for their education and remained to enrich letters, the sciences and, in short, the intellectual life of the metropolis, was by no means small. Brazil found compensation for this loss of her sons by giving to the life of Portugal, at least to that of the Court, some peculiar and foreign features which extended to the various classes of society.

I consider that Spain's colonists took a smaller part in the development of the mother country previous to the independence of the New World, than did those of Portugal, largely due to the fact that the Spanish colonies had their own universities, as well as to the geographical situation of the colonies in reference to their respective mother countries. It is obvious that comunication between the Spanish ports of Seville and Cadiz on the one hand and the regions of the River Plate, of the Pacific and even of the Antilles on the other was much more difficult than the relatively short and easy voyage from Lisbon to Brazil, and vice versa, with stops at Madeira and the Azores and continent of Africa. The American continent, in the southern hemisphere and in its eastern coast, advances, so to speak, in search of the civilization of the Old World; the configuration of the Gulf of Mexico to be sure gives at first glance the contrary impression, but this geographical accident did not prevent the establishment of a close and constant administrative and economic connection, and did not make the number of colonists who visited Europe in any way inconsiderable.

Simon Bolívar was, as the son of a noble family, the playfellow at Aránjuez of the Prince of the Asturias, afterwards Ferdinand VII, that King of Spain whom he was to despoil of a large part of his colonial dominions; at Paris he associated with scientists such as Humboldt and Bonpland; he was present at the crowning of Napoleon at Milan as King of Italy, and in a burst of enthusiasm for classical history, went to take the oath on the Aventine that he would devote his life to the freeing of his continent.

Miranda [6] reveals himself to us as even more of a cosmopolitan. A military participant in your War of Independence, he appears later as a freemason in England, as the guest of the great Catherine in Russia, as a superior officer under Dumouriez, the conqueror at the battles of Valmy and Jemmapes—events which ushered in the heroic period of the French revolutionary expansion in Europe. The masonic lodge established by Miranda in London for the purpose of securing the political emancipation of the continent which was still in bondage, extended its ramifications as far as Brazil, which hitherto had been widely separated from the Spanish American world. This lodge thus became an influential factor in the revolt of Pernambuco in 1817 [7], which even during the residence of Dom John VI in Brazil, seriously imperiled the Portuguese dominions in America.[1]

Rapid then, as you see—for what are three centuries in universal history—had been the evolution of this new Latin American world, which, in the first half of the sixteenth century, could only offer the spectacle of iniquitous and deadly combats between the invaders and the natives, and which, now in the beginning of the nineteenth century, was already proclaiming its rights to self-government and autonomy, or was serving as a refuge for an entire Court of Europe, fleeing in terror from Napoleon, the seat of a colonial administration becoming naturally the capital of a vast monarchy [8].

It is true that only a limited group of men of culture were advocating those rights of freedom and self-government and that the great mass of the people of these countries do not have, even to-day, a satisfactory notion of any *social contract*. But does not the same thing happen in other countries? And even in those nations which march in the vanguard of civilization will the minority cease to have charge of the administration of public affairs? Comparatively speaking, it may even be said that the culture of the Latin American colonies at that time was superior, in certain respects, to that of the Anglo-American colonies, whose development today astonishes the world. On the other hand you gained much ground and outdistanced us all, after you had secured your independence: which certainly signifies that the race, the environment and the time had not equally prepared us for the conscientious direction of our destinies.

The race showed the effect of the physical and moral union. Sr. Lacerda, in the paper to which I have already referred, although recognizing the accidental superiority of some mulattoes and half-caste over the original factors or parents, points out that as a whole the legacy from the negro race was unfortunate. This legacy consists, in his opinion, of de-

---

[1] It will be recalled that King John VI resided in Brazil from 1808 to 1821.

fects of language, vices of blood, wrong conceptions of life and death, gross superstitions, fetishism, and a total lack of comprehension of every lofty sentiment of honor and of human dignity. The picture will appear darkly colored or not, according to each one's preferences or prejudices; in any case, he failed to mention that the moral influence of Europe was so powerful, even upon the product of the intermarriage, that the most astute politician of the last years of the Brazilian Empire was a mulatto, as was also the most delicate, the most subtle, in fine, the most Athenian writer recorded in the literary annals of the country. Of mixed blood also was Gonçalves Diaz, Brazil's greatest poet and one of the great American lyrists,—an artist of vivid imagination, of rich coloring, wonderful rhythm and profound sensibility, whose mission it was to recall the native traditions of the country and idealize the soul of its aboriginal population.

These superior minds, animating bodies in whose veins circulated the blood of the so-called inferior races, are the best testimony to the efficiency of crossing ideas. Moreover, if physical crossing leaves its impress, why should not the crossing of mental or moral qualities leave its effect also? And if this can be exercised in the direction of deterioration, why would it not be exercised also in the opposite direction of elevation? The instances I have cited are only a few among hundreds which may be seen by any one who will look for them in Latin America.

The local *milieu* was suffering, it is true, from great violence and tyranny: the conquerors were prodigal of both, as invaders of any kind are apt to be. On account of the inequality in education and, consequently, of the difference in intellectual viewpoint, the moment of emancipation was one of insufficient harmony between the elements destined to live together. Nevertheless in insisting upon the first point, it would be permitted to ask if instead of occupying ourselves with the past, that is, with trying to explain by means of history and tradition what has been the political and moral evolution of Latin America compared with Anglo-Saxon America, we should face the future, which of the policies followed is the wise one?

Will not the practical method which, during the colonial period and later during the period of independence, the sons of the Iberian Peninsula unconsciously took to solve the problem of the races, perchance facilitate its solution, or rather, will it not assure its solution in the future? Indeed, in your country, which is in so many ways the most progressive in the world, and the one in which the greatest progress has already been made toward the regulation of ethical problems, this racial question continues pressing, inciting to acts of violence which you, whom I may call the intellectuals and the disciples of philosophers, are the first to deplore and condemn. Yet we of Latin America have already settled this same problem in the most satisfactory manner by fusion, a fusion in which the inferior elements will shortly disappear. Thus, when mulattoes and half castes shall no longer exist among us, when the negro or Indian blood shall have become diluted in European blood, which in times past and not far distant—it must not be forgotten—received its contingents of Berbers, Numidians, Tartars and other races, you will be threatened with preserving indefinitely within your confines irreducible populations, of diverse color and hostile sentiments.

I will not say that the general tone of your culture has not gained by this aloofness of the races, by the consequent integrity of the purity of the white race which has contributed so greatly to the present superiority of your civilization; but the situation created by antagonism, that is, by the presence of two or more races which do not fuse, will some day have to have its *dénoument*, and the *dénoument* brought about by love is always preferable to that which is the result of hate.

This rule of love followed by the Latin peoples of America does not date from to-day; it was always identical in its spirit, even when the times were less inclined to moral considerations. The *Leyes de Indias* [10] (Laws of the Indies) are, in the opinion of Don Vicente G. Quesada, a writer who does not hesitate to censure the faults of the Spanish colonial policy, much superior to the contemporary laws of other nations, revealing a constant lofty purpose on the part of the administration of the mother country in favor of her American colonies.

This does not mean, however, that these laws were superior to their epoch, "whose standards in their entirety they adopted, without suspecting perhaps that posterity would regard them as backward and pernicious." It means only that the more affectionate, or if you prefer the term, the more expansive nature of the southern race perfected that aspect of their legislation. The natives were, it is true, badly treated, violated, enslaved by the conquerors from the Iberian Peninsula, but, as I have already pointed out to you, by the side of these exploiters, from the first hour, were missionaries of the same nationality, contending with them for this new portion of humanity in order to elevate it by education and precept. With admirable zeal these missionaries set to work immediately to learn the American languages, and while acquiring them they even went so far, in Mexico, as to invent figures, after the manner of the local hieroglyphics, in order to inculcate thoroughly the rudiments of the Christian doctrine.

The foundation of the Seminary of San José, a primary school and an ecclesiastical professional institute for Indian children, was almost contemporaneous with the conquest of the Mexican territory from the Aztecs. The College of Santa Cruz de Tlatelolco furnished Indian teachers for the children of the Spaniards. This college was founded in 1536, by the virtuous bishop Zumárraga, whose splendid biography by Garcia Icazbalceta you would greatly enjoy reading [11]. In 1553, there was established a home for foundlings for the unfortunate offspring of the temporary unions of Spanish soldiers with Indian women, the support of natural children being obligatory, however, whenever it was possible to establish the paternity. The Viceroy, Antonio de Mendoza [12], whose task it was to put into effect the Royal decree authorizing the establishment of this home, was also the founder of a retreat for girls of mixed blood, where they received some education before leaving the institution to marry.

In these very brief pedagogical and philanthropical references I confine myself to Mexico, your adjoining neighbor, and to the sixteenth century, the century of the discoveries and first explorations, in order not to extend a list which you might think interminable. But any one who will acquaint himself with the subject will conclude that, notwithstanding the many adverse influences, charity, the foundation *par excellence* of our Christian civilization, no less than the benefits of education, reached the Latin section of the New World earlier than it did the Anglo-Saxon section.

Neither can it be doubted that at the close of the colonial period in America our culture was, if not more solid, at least more brilliant than yours; our social life was more ostentatious, if not more civilized; our development was fuller and freer, if not more fruitful.

It will suffice to remind you, as regards Brazil, that in Minas Geraes, whose gold and diamonds were making Portugal the wonder of Europe, lyric poetry at the end of the eighteenth century acquired a natural feeling and an almost romantic expression of a personal character which make the poetry of the colonial period decidedly superior to the neoclassic conventionality of the mother country. It will be sufficient to tell you that the luxury of your Virginia could not compare with the splendor, somewhat ostentatious but suggestive, of the "Captaincy of Gold," and especially to remind you that the winning of the West, which in the United States was the feature of the nineteenth century, was in the case of Brazil begun by our pioneers in the sixteenth century, and was already concluded in the eighteenth century.

The great results obtained by our diplomacy in fixing Brazil's boundaries with the neighboring countries—a task sufficiently complicated, for Brazil borders on all the countries and colonies of South America, except Chile—are, with the exception of slight modifications due to geographical corrections rather than to political motives, nothing more than the confirmation of treaties concluded between Spain and Portugal in 1750 and 1777. These treaties, in their turn, represented the international recognition of Portugal's conquest of territory beyond the line traced in the fifteenth century by the Papal Bull and the Treaty of Tordesillas, which theoretically reconciled the Cortes of Madrid and Lisbon [13].

The desire for expansion, identical with that which led the Portuguese adventurers to cross the mountains of the eastern coast of the southern continent and to explore the rivers of the plateau to their central headwaters, led the Spanish adventurers to subjugate Mexico and to radiate from there to Florida, to New Mexico, California and Guatemala, that is, to the east, north and south; to spread themselves along the coasts of the Pacific, soon after this Southern Sea had been discovered by Nuñez de Balboa; to take possession of the immense backbone of South America, occupying the Andes wherever there were outcroppings of silver lodes and establishing settlements even at points which were without any attractions whatever; and finally to penetrate into the southeast as far as the pampas, in their quest for precious metals.

It was this same desire for colonial expansion of the two Iberian countries which led to the political and economic organization of the new nationalities for which the territorial conquest opened the way; the initial cell of this organization will be found in an old Roman municipal institution transplanted to America by the founders of the new Latin World.

The municipal chambers of Brazil and the *cabildos,* or municipal corporations, of Spanish America, were indeed the colonial nurseries of liberal ideas and rights; however much the shadow of royal despotism might obscure them, depriving them of the radiant light of liberty, they constituted the soil in which those rights germinated and where they finally burst into blossom. These corporations were popular in their character, and in many cases also in their composition, although the legislation of this period and particularly that of a later period greatly changed their nature. They had been granted by Spain and Portugal to their possessions in the sixteenth century when such organizations, as appears from the relative autonomy they enjoyed, still had a significance and a reality in the Peninsula. And despite the obstacles which the throne placed in the way of their development they continued to progress through the force of their own momentum.

In Spain there had even been a time when, as one writer has expressed it, by the side of the landed feudalism there existed a kind of urban feudalism extending its influence over towns and villages and having as its basis the large number of communes, especially those created in the territory won from the Moors. In Portugal the *foraes* or charters of the municipal councils no longer contained their former privileges, which had been as great as the Spanish, and, like them, were given as a recompense for services rendered in the wars against the Mohammedans; but the inhabitants or citizens of these municipal towns continued to be the raw material for parliamentary representation, since it was they who furnished the taxes until the Crown absorbed all rights and privileges.

On the other side of the ocean, far from the supreme power, which in the pursuit of its ideal of its own preponderant authority was encroaching upon their rights, the municipal chambers instinctively resisted whenever possible, and sometimes even beyond their strength, the authority of the feudal lords, governors and viceroys which had been made despotic by law and which aimed to become even more tyrannical in practice. If perchance these chambers did not find sufficient authority for this opposition in the legislation which swathed them in the cradle, or the traditions of the Peninsula did not permit it—for in Europe the nobility and later the King constantly opposed the municipal corporations—they at times necessarily found in the colonies conditions of anarchy sufficient to justify their disregard of the text of the Constitution.

Castillo de Bobadilla [14], a Spanish publicist who preceded the writers on European public law—I say European because an American public law has been invented, though in what respect it differs from the other I could not say—goes so far as to find a precedent in republican and imperial Rome for the full meetings of the *vecindario*, that is, the popular assembly called *"cabildo abierto"* in which the ediles and electors were associated, thus corresponding in a certain sense to your primary meeting. The Roman precedent refers to the occasional admission to the Senate of knights (equites) and other supernumerary persons who had held the office of magistrate, or other citizens chosen by the censors for consultation and counsel in grave business matters.

The political and social importance of the typical Spanish municipal institution, or rather of the Neo-Latin institution, transplanted to the

New World, has been the subject of wide discussion, and the pendulum of opinion has swung and continues to swing between those who assert that in the colonial *cabildos,* which were created for the government and good administration of justice of the new American cities, there resided, in law and in fact, popular sovereignty, and those who do not see in them anything more than the "sad parody" of the Spanish councils which were overthrown by Charles V, after the famous revolt of the *Communeros* [15].

The functions of these *cabildos* were, as you may imagine in view of the precision which characterized the Spanish bureaucracy, of which the *Rey papelista,*[2] as Canovas del Castillo [16] called Philip II, was the most perfect representative, minutely set forth in the Laws of the Indies. They included, in addition to the services common to all edileships, administrative and judicial functions. In their judicial capacity the *cabildos* acted in certain cases on gifts of lands, decided lawsuits, and even constituted in civil matters up to a certain point, a court of second instance.

But just as in your constitutional system,—the so-called American presidential system which Brazil imported when she established the Republican form of Government and which other Latin American countries had adopted before her,—there was an executive magistrate with full powers alongside of the deliberative body; so, alongside or rather above the Roman Senate, there was the Emperor. Only, in the case of the *cabildos,* the *corregidor,* or chief civil magistrate who carried out their resolutions, was appointed by the king, and not elected by the people. This fundamental defect, which was common to the *cabildo,* would be enough to prevent it from being the practical school of democracy which some would like to regard it. To begin with, it lacked the essential, a representative basis, the people taking no part in it, either at the time of its establishment—for the first council was directly appointed by the Governor—or afterward, as the *regidores,* or administrative officers, elected their own successors. In time even this form of election was largely done away with, as the result of the aldermen ceding their staff of office for a pecuniary consideration, which was the source of many grave abuses [17].

Moreover, the revenues of these corporations were small, their taxing power was limited, and ordinarily they enjoyed but little prestige. This fact was due in part to the despotic tendencies of the governors and military commanders, encouraged, as a South American writer has pointed

---

[2] This expression might perhaps be translated "The king submerged in state papers."

out, by the great distance from the metropolis and the corrupt Spanish administration. Nevertheless, it is a fact, as the historical critic, Dr. Jose Salgado [18] of the University of Montevideo, has indicated, that the colonists were permitted to take part in the communal deliberation by means of the open *cabildos,* already mentioned, which were sometimes convoked by the municipal corporations and at other times by spontaneous agreement of the citizens in order to decide matters of grave importance. In these open meetings the opinions of all were heard and their votes affected the deliberations taken.

It must not be forgotten that the municipal corporations of the colonies were concessions of the crown, granted with the object of fostering the colonization of the possessions which the navigators and discoverers had added to its dominion, and of promoting the constitutional organization of these distant sections of the metropolis, connected by a common sovereignty. In Spain the *fueros* or royal grants represented rather the recognition by the throne of a state of things brought about by the difficulties of the Christian reconquest; they were a sort of free contract of mutual respect and defense.

It is not surprising, therefore, that these Spanish municipal charters, the oldest recorded in the political history of Europe since the fall of the Roman Empire and the invasion of the barbarians, should guard so zealously the prerogatives of the burghers that they denied to the lords the right to build castles in the territory of the communes, and made the nobility and people equal before the civil law. The *fuero* of Palencia, for example, expressly stated that there could only be two palaces within the confines of the city, that of the king and that of the bishop, and that there was to be no distinction between the houses of the rich and of the poor.

It is well known that in those times, which were really more tolerant and liberal than those which followed, the Jews were allowed to establish themselves in the towns with the enjoyment of the ordinary rights and privileges, and the personal guarantees of the inhabitants of the councils were such that no citizen could be punished without having first been heard and condemned. Only a judicial sentence could authorize the confiscation of property, and the Cortes alone had the right to impose extraordinary taxes.

I do not wish, however, to compare the colonial *cabildos* with the old communes of Castile and Aragon of the time of the *fueros,* or with the free English communes which were later revived and flourished among you, but to call your attention to the tradition which they represented, although imperfectly, and to the importance which they eventually assumed. "Some of these," writes Dr. J. Salgado, "in spite of the laws of their organization and the attempts made by the Spanish authorities to absorb them, were gradually acquiring a real autonomy which later converted them into corporations openly revolutionary."

This was the case with the *Cabildo* of Montevideo, at the time of the occupation of Buenos Aires by the English expedition, in 1806. In order to enable the natives to reconquer the territory which had been taken from them, the *Cabildo* of Montevideo raised the governor to the post of supreme chief, giving him full authority, for they considered that the viceroy had rendered himself unworthy of the office through his cowardly desertion of the field of combat. By this act, the wishes of the people were not only placed above the laws and the decrees of the sovereign, but as the voluntary expression of the people were ruthlessly carried out. And when on the other side of the La Plata estuary the liberation of Argentina was proclaimed, the *Cabildo* of Buenos Aires, although constrained and coerced, served nevertheless the group of liberal-minded men as an instrument for effecting the revolution within the law.

The separation of Uruguay from Spain and its independent organization which followed close upon that of Argentina were effected by the same method, which we may call the revolutionary-legal method. General Mitre [19], soldier, writer and distinguished statesman, who deserved the title of the GRAND OLD MAN of Argentina, has justly pointed out that at Montevideo were enacted the two principal scenes of the democratic drama of Independence: the open *cabildo* and the establishment of a self-governing *junta,* or board, appointed by the people.

You see, therefore, that in the evolution of your government the fundamental principle is identical with ours and it must not be forgotten that even in monarchical Brazil the Empire sprang from a movement of concentration on the part of the provincial *juntas,* elected by popular vote, and that its proclamation and, later, its organization, had had to be ratified by the municipalities—a significant homage paid to popular sovereignty.

Under the circumstances it is not at all surprising that after an existence through three centuries of colonial expansion this old Latin and later neo-Iberian institution—despite the fact that in many cases it had been nurtured in a hothouse atmosphere—should play a role of great importance in that period of transition signalized by the Wars of Independence. In the general confusion caused by the political upheaval and the spirit of the century the *cabildos* assumed an authority which no other institution was capable of wielding. Under the pretext of guarding the integrity and inviolability of the royal rights of their direct suzerain, the legitimate king of Spain, these corporations in fact took away the possessions of the crown, not only from the jurisdiction of the foreign king and usurper, but from all attempts at authority sent from Europe.

In Brazil, where the presence of the monarch prevented an exhibition of this pretense of colonial loyalty—whose sincerity, except perhaps at the outset, was open to serious question—the municipal chambers soon took a conspicuous part, and one in keeping with their character. This happened at the time of the conflict between the national regency left by Dom John VI, in the person of Dom Pedro the Prince Royal, who was afterwards proclaimed the first constitutional Emperor of Brazil, and the constituent Cortes of Lisbon, which sought to reduce the colonial kingdom which was already enjoying autonomy—for Portugal and Brazil had formed a united kingdom since 1816—to its former colonial condition of unequivocal servitude.

It was at this juncture, as I have just said, that the municipal chambers of Brazil, giving expression to the local resistance which was fortunately becoming national owing to the presence in the country of the throne, which acted as a center of attraction, sought to establish Dom Pedro permanently in his supreme post upon the ampler foundation of the provincial boards, giving him at first the title and honor of "perpetual defender of Brazil," and later the rank and dignity of sovereign. It was those corporations, therefore, that, displaying the greatest wisdom and without shedding any blood whatsoever, brought about the independence of the country. The municipal chamber of Rio de Janeiro, in particular, took the most active part in the establishment of the democratic empire that Brazil came to be and remained. In a certain sense it may be said that it initiated the movement [20].

The methods by which political emancipation was secured in Brazil differed from those employed in Spanish America chiefly in this: our independence was accomplished, so to speak, without war—for this term can hardly be applied to the few spasmodic attempts at resistance which were promptly crushed. And the bloodless character of the revolution was due primarily to the existence in Brazil of a legitimately and traditionally constituted government which served as a shield against revolutionary aspirations, and which enjoyed the respect and sympathy of the majority. Consequently it succeeded in overpowering its enemies, that is, those who, fascinated by the mirage of republicanism, opposed the monarchical régime in principle.

Any discussion of the political emancipation of Brazil must necessarily take into account the influence of the Regent, Dom Pedro [21], in whom all dreams of independence were led to concentrate. On account of his close connection with the throne of the metropolis, of whose reigning dynasty he was the most direct representative after the monarch, he not only commended himself to a people which had only just emerged—if we may employ the metaphor—from its chrysalis state, but thanks to the prestige which monarchical institutions still enjoyed in the mother country he succeeded in imposing himself, if not on the respect, at all events on other less patent sentiments of such reforming Cortes, as those of Lisbon, which declared themselves liberal without being revolutionary.

Turning to the other section of Latin America it cannot be denied that as the result of the longer sustained efforts and the greater violence with which the separation was effected, the Spanish ex-colonies were able to surpass the kingdom of Brazil in the mighty work of political and social reconstruction after independence had been won. Without any agreement among themselves, each one legislating in its own special interest, they changed in the same way the constitutional structure from its foundation, establishing not only freedom of industry, of trade, of colonization and of religion—all of which Brazil had obtained from the transplanted royalty as spontaneous grants, although they naturally were still subject to certain restrictions, due to prejudices of the time and surroundings—but also decreeing the general extinction of slavery, the abolishment of the Indian tribute and the suppression of the nobility.

I have already spoken of the painful birth of the idea of emancipation of the negro in the United States and Spanish America. It was a freedom won by blood, Brazil being the only country in which it was effected peacefully, by evolution, amid the rejoicings of the people, who felt that the institution of slavery was incompatible with their state of civilization. And it cannot be said that with the exception of this social institution, which morally did not last any longer among us than it did in fact among you—for the act of 1863 was the death-knell of slavery in the rest of America where this scourge existed—human progress was not equal in the two sections of Latin America.

The extinction of the Inquisition, that executioner of thought; the freedom of the press; the regulation of the monastical communities; the reduction of ecclesiastical privileges and consequent lessening of the religious power; the abolition of a few burdensome taxes; the reform of the civil, commercial and penal laws;—all of these conquests of the uprising in the Spanish colonies were, in Brazil, obtained by that same process of evolution which, before the separation, reflected the wave of constitutional reform sweeping over Portugal, and which, also, after the separation of the two kingdoms, was the result of the establishment of the representative régime.

This régime synchronized with political emancipation and its acclimatization earlier would not have been in harmony with the conditions then prevailing; but even so one must seek in the past of the Latin-American countries the tradition for all that occurred later in this connection. I mentioned a little while ago that the most attractive feature of the Spanish civilization, or rather of the Iberian civilization in the New World, was its sympathy for the natives, a sympathy which did not prevent abuses, acts of violence, persecutions and tyrannies; for there were all of these, and, unfortunately, not on a small scale. Yet this sympathy included a progressive and regenerative element which was the result of an instinctive feeling of the spiritual equality of that alien race, of a sense of the iniquity of treating them in any other way than with justice and benevolence, and of the recognition of the right of that inferior people to intellectual and moral education and to social elevation.

We have already seen that in Spanish America—and the same conditions held in Portuguese America—the schools and colleges for Indians and their descendants were contemporaneous with those established for the white children of the European colonists. This idea of establishing schools on the heels of the conquest was not as chimerical as might appear at first sight. Rather is one amazed at the number and importance of these institutions considering the period and the local conditions. The province of New Granada, now Colombia, which in her highlands was the least accessible of the Spanish possessions and had comparatively the smallest resources, counted in the seventeenth century twenty-three colleges, not including the primary schools which existed in nearly all the convents. It should be added that many of these primary schools as well as colleges were due to private initiative.

In Latin-American countries, education, as well as charity, has always been favored in a high degree by legacies and donations. In a city like that of Rio de Janeiro, for example, which has at the present time nearly a million inhabitants, the public charity service is scarcely done by the city administration at all, but almost entirely, and in a manner eminently satisfactory, by that rich old colonial institution, the *Misericordia,* the first *Misericordias* in Portugal having been established in the fifteenth century. This institution has hospitals for the sick, maternity and children's wards, provides for the burial of the dead, and guards cemeteries.

Naturally, the Government has always looked with favor upon this prosperous institution which was working totally in its interest. This was not the case, however, with the strictly ecclesiastical donations. These conduced to the wealth and consequent influence of the religious communities, which, by means of this material prestige, were able to enter into conflicts with the civil authorities. Certain disagreements between viceroys and bishops, as well as between bishops and Jesuits, remained famous in the colonial annals. The anecdotal history of the New World of Latin America is as interesting and as diverting as yours, if not more so; you can become acquainted with a part of it, and that the most curious, by reading the *Tradiciones del Peru,* by Ricardo Palma [22].

Education in the Iberian colonies, as I have already pointed out, was of an essentially religious character, for it was ecclesiastical in its origin, and even served as a pretext for the emulation of the various Catholic congregations, especially in the Spanish possessions, where the Jesuits, Dominicans, and Franciscans, contended for the educational monopoly. This rivalry, however, could only find vent within the prescribed limits; and, as Don Vicente Quesada [23] well says, since there was no place in the monotonous existence of the colony for political strifes, all the activities were concentrated in these academic contests. "The refined, scholarly and somewhat mandarinic culture resulting from these contests imparted to the Latin-American people, isolated as they were from the rest of the world, a characteristic polish as rhetoricians, formulists, controversialists, erudite scholars devoted to beauty of style, observers of outward forms and conventions, sophists, prone to attach too great importance to words, and especially much given to an affected ergotism."

In the same spirit as this admirable observation of the eminent Argentine just cited are the words of Juan and Ulloa [24] with regard to the effects of ecclesiastical education. These distinguished naval officers accompanied the French Scientific Mission on its expedition to South America, which had been made possible by the fact that the princes of the house of Bourbon were seated on the thrones of Spain and France. They observed that the educated youth of the colonies, who were truly gifted with remarkable cleverness and rare powers of quick assimilation, were notable for their knowledge of philosophy, of theology and even of jurisprudence, but that they lacked acquaintance with the political, historical and natural sciences.

The worst feature, however, of these Latin-American colonial societies, which were without horizons of their own—for they enjoyed neither industrial nor commercial freedom—was their administrative incapacity; rather I should say their enforced inability to govern themselves, or, in other words, their need of political education. It was in these respects that you showed your great superiority over us, a superiority which enabled you to make rapid advancement after you had gained your independence. Among you, established tradition had only to continue under a new name and under more favorable conditions. The government was in fact already in the hands of the colonists and their descendants. We, on the other hand, had to adapt ourselves to the changed conditions, whereas among you the adaption had already been made.

The two civilizations, though, had one characteristic in common which tended to favor and really did favor our progress. This was Particularism, whose influence is seen in all the various aspects of the evolution of America, both Iberian and Anglo-Saxon America. Where one least expects to find it, it rises up, to explain, if not to justify the march of events, or as an artist would say, to fix the different planes in a sketch of culture. Let us take, for example, what was the greatest political and social problem of the New World, that is, slavery, a thing of the past and yet of the present, for its consequences have not yet ceased to be felt, its vestiges are far from having disappeared. The institution of slavery had its best guarantee in its diffusion: it was identified with our evolution and had become an institution common to all American colonies, passing naturally to the new countries of all nationalities. It is evident that with its continuance assured in the United States, there was no reason for it not to continue in the other countries of the continent where slavery had resisted the emancipation crises, namely Brazil, Cuba, Porto Rico and the Guianas. Of these countries, Brazil alone had achieved independence.

The "peculiar institution" received from your solid South tacit but effective moral support, and with us in Brazil, in the same way as among you, although not in the same degree, it derived encouragement from the autonomy of the states or provinces, as they were then called. In Brazil, this political spirit of particularism continued to exist even under a policy of centralization: it was favored moreover, by the great difference in the economic conditions of the provinces, which enabled some of them to free their small number of slaves, like Ceará and Amazonas, while others, like São Paulo and Pernambuco, clung to a state of things which they regarded as inseparable from their prosperity.

It was this centralization of power brought about by the monarchy which enabled the abolition of slavery in Brazil to be effected without bloodshed or civil strife, for it may be said that a sectional line was being established in the country between the provinces which had slaves and those which no longer had them—although it did not offer the geometrical precision of the line drawn between your North and South—and that, there as here, the abolitionists began their active crusade in the midst of the same prejudices and rancors.

The correction, or rather, the result of Particularism is Federalism, a word which stands out large in the political lexicon of our double continent. You are preëminently the country of Federalism—a country of adoption like all those of the New World—but historical probity obliges me to state, and in so doing I may possibly wound your vanity (a vanity which would be entirely justified), that Brazilian Federalism was not, as one might at first suppose, through a false deduction based on coincidence, an application of the principle which had been so successful in the constitutional organization of the United States.

Federalism in Brazil has passed through many phases and vicissitudes. In 1822 it was necessarily and advantageously sacrificed to the national unity, but in 1834 it had returned with sufficient vitality to compel the acceptance of the Additional Act to the Imperial Constitution of 1825, an Act prepared under the Regency and favoring decentralization, and which in 1889 served as a model for the organization of the Republic. Yet this same federal principle has not only struck its roots as deep as a history which is but four centuries old will permit, but its origin is to be found in a past still more remote. For we must never forget that the history of Latin America is nothing more than that of the Iberian Peninsula transplanted to a new scene in which new human elements take part, and one must seek in the environment and traditions of Europe for the thread of its institutions and of its ideals.

Throughout America, however, we find that particularism is the political feature of the last century, that is, of the century immediately following independence, in striking contrast to Europe, where the policy of nationalities, with its necessary corollary of unification, has been the dominant one from Napoleon's time to Bismarck's. In South America, Bolívar was unable to bring together in a constitutional whole the different although homogeneous parts of the Empire which had been severed by historical events and conflicting aspirations. He was obliged to separate the *Audiencia* of Charcas and raise it to the dignity of a nation under his own name; he was unable to maintain the Presidency of Quito either as a part of independent Peru or of Great Colombia which he had founded, and he died at the moment when Great Colombia again definitely separated into Venezuela and New Granada. In North America a gigantic struggle was opened between the Northern and Southern States for the purpose of severing the Union which so many battle-fields had cemented. While these events took place in North and South America, in Europe cruel and bloody wars were being waged for the purpose of reconstructing, or perhaps it would be more accurate to say, for the purpose of constructing the unity of Italy, Dante's cherished dream, and the unity of Germany, which the survival of German feudalism has prevented up to our time.

In the New World, truly, the constitutional ideal lent itself to various interpretations. I do not need to remind you here in the United States of Jefferson and the Republicans, of Calhoun and the Democrats, of Jefferson Davis and the Confederates. Today even the rights of the states are frequently invoked and defended, although it is no longer desired to convert their autonomy into independence. In Latin America, we see that the centrifugal movement was also the initial one, for all the genius of Bolívar could not avail to prevent its spread throughout the former colonies of Spain. It would have been necessary to have established a throne, as in Brazil, in order to maintain or create the splendid unity which circumstances of language, or religion, of customs and of sentiments favored, but which was opposed by circumstances, no less strong, of history, geography and political imagination.

The plan of Bolívar, like that of the American Federalists, had been to place the power of the compound above the autonomy of the parts, to sacrifice particularist interests to the interests of the whole which was superior to them. He therefore began by respecting in the territorial demarcation of freed Spanish America, the principle of *uti possidetis juris*, which was the only reasonable and logical foundation he could give this political division, and even so it did not become exempt from difficulties and conflicts such as those which have appeared among almost all, if not all, the Latin Republics of the New World.

You all surely remember the boundary disputes between Chile and Argentina, which were settled by the awards of the King of England and of one of your diplomats; the dispute between Argentina and Paraguay, which was decided by President Hayes; the controversy between Bolivia and Peru over the Acre Territory, acquired by Brazil, which was decided by the President of Argentina; the dispute between Venezuela and Colombia, which was submitted to the Queen Regent of Spain; and the disputes still pending between Peru, Colombia, and Ecuador, not to cite others.

Bolívar's ultimate conception, which rested on the military hegemony of Colombia—a state which he had called into being—included, as a necessary complement, the principle of arbitration for the regulation of differences between countries. In extolling and advocating this principle, he left the narrow sphere of patriotism—which was really an *esprit de clocher* in the divided Spanish America—in order to enter the higher sphere of international harmony.

Thus was formed what a Colombian writer has justly termed the international ideal of Bolívar, founded on tradition and a safe basis, therefore, for the codification of public law, which is being proposed by the governments for the people of this hemisphere. And this noble inclination would of itself be enough to doom to oblivion the faults of this great man:—his ambition for personal and autocratic rule; the pretorian spirit which he was largely responsible for infiltrating into the Spanish-American political organism; his imperialism disguised under the cloak of the unity of the race.

As it often happens, however, with social events, the results in this case went far beyond mere personal advantage, the work of the Liberator becoming truly rich in fruits, since his ardent desire for the preponderance of Colombia and his monocratic tendencies indirectly assured, before the Monroe Doctrine, the safety of the independence of the other Republics, through the extension of the military activities which broke the Spanish resistance beyond their original orbit.

We shall see, too, that in the mind of Bolívar the thought for self was never unaccompanied by general ideas or conceptions of public order. But we must first examine the evolution, in America, of the federative principle, which has been its chief political characteristic. As early as 1815, when the hero of Spanish America wandered, an exile, though not hopeless, over the Antilles, he saw in Panamá, whose Isthmus you are soon going to open to the world's commerce, the Corinth of the new Hellenic Confederation, the seat of a political and military league governed by an international assembly of plenipotentiaries, like the Achean League of Greece. The Macedonian influence, and later the Roman, against which that Confederation was warned, finds its modern counterpart in the influence of Europe, against whose influence it was Bolívar's idea to oppose the American political body "with an aspect of majesty and grandeur," as he said, "unparalleled among the ancient nations."

LECTURE III.

Origin of the federative principle.—Local government and administrative centralization in Portuguese and Spanish America: their different aspects.—Lack of uniformity in colonial legislation.—Viceroys and *Audiencias*.—Union through confederation in the three Americas.—Schemes of American royalties: Aranda, Pitt and Chateaubriand.—The monarchical idea in Latin America and its moral effect.—The first Monroe Doctrine.—Franco-British rivalries in the course of the eighteenth and nineteenth centuries.—Napoleon and the British interests in the New World.—Monarchical possibilities in Buenos Aires, Mexico, and Colombia.—Pitiable rôle of Ferdinand VII.—Iturbide, Bolívar, and San Martin.—European or creole dynasties.—Historical function of the Brazilian Empire.—The moderate minds in the colonies and liberal ideas in Spain.—Precedents for the idea of separation.—The traditional discontent, the genesis of the patriotic instinct, and the personal tie between the sovereign and his possessions in America.

WE have now to examine the precedents for federation, to discover the genesis of the idea of particularism, to search for the earliest traditions of local government, whether established under the influence of the metropolis, or due to the spontaneous action of the elements transplanted from Europe to a different environment.

Of the two Iberian kingdoms Portugal alone, with the design of a speedier occupation and a surer defense of the new dominion beyond the sea, restored, in Brazil, the old and already abolished feudal system. The South American colony was divided into feudal captaincies, and distributed, in the first half of the sixteenth century, among a few lords of the court and some high officials, to whom as donataries the king granted the most extensive powers, reserving only for himself the rights of suzerain; for instance, the supreme bestowal of justice in certain cases, and the collection of taxes.

Though the inefficiency of such a constitutional system was soon recognized and its anachronism was patent, the fundamental principle remained more or less operative during the colonial epoch; it did not even disappear after the establishment of Independence and continues to act as a political pendulum. It was true that the centralization attempted in the colony a short time after that essay of territorial partition, was so to speak illusory, although Spain strengthened it at the time of her union with Portugal.

During this union of the Iberian kingdoms the Spanish government, always in favor of a policy of centralization, dared to deprive the local chiefs—the governors we may say, as in 1580 there were almost no donataries left in Brazil—of their judicial attributes. Centralization continued however to prove illusory, because the captain-generals were in fact independent of the governor-general, who was invested later on with the title of viceroy.

The German professor Handelmann [1], who keeps his place as our best foreign historian—less dramatic and attractive than Southey [2], but never surpassed in interesting documentation and philosophical insight—admirably pointed out this characteristic of Brazilian evolution. Besides, the unifying work of Spain, followed out as it was in a more vigorous and effective way, was abruptly checked by the Dutch war, which caused Portugal the temporary loss of the enormous territory from the São Francisco river up to the Amazon, one-half, perhaps, of the Brazils then explored. After the reëstablishment of Portuguese authority and the recovery of the whole of her American colonies, the Lisbon government did not continue the centralizing policy pursued by Spain, either through lack of energy, or owing to doubt as to the efficacy of the Spanish system. Each captaincy remained an administrative unit, directly and individually subject to the orders of the metropolis, without any intervention from the royal representative, although his nominal power extended over the whole of the possessions of the New World. Each of these captaincies lived its own life, more or less as independent of its neighbors, very much as did the English colonies of North America.[1]

Portugal was so much more in a position to restore feudalism in America and then to create amongst her possessions an organic particularism, owing to the fact that she had rapidly attained a remarkable degree of political and social cohesion. In the mother country the provinces were mere administrative divisions, only differentiated by the picturesque costumes of the people. This result had immediately followed the conquest of the land over the Moors and the superposition of the King, helped by the commons, over the nobility which in other countries had been so much opposed to the work of national unification.

In Spain the process of national growth was somewhat different. Her

---

[1] This point is admirably discussed by M. Charles de Lannoy, a professor in the University of Ghent, in p. 94 of the work written in collaboration with M. Herman Vander Linden entitled "Histoire de l'Expansion coloniale des Peuples européens." (Bruxelles, 1907.) The first section of this work deals with the colonies of Portugal, the latter with those of Spain.

territorial integration took place but late[2]—on the eve, we may say, of her maritime expansion—and even so it proved incomplete and precarious, as such unification consisted chiefly in the union of two royal houses, the Castilian and the Aragonese. Each group of states maintained their peculiar institutions within their respective boundaries, and their inhabitants, as well, preserved marked differences of character and civilization—differences which may also be accounted for in part by the disparity of geographical conditions. This is why federalism in Spain today is so logical and legitimate an expression of public aspirations, and why Pi y Margall's book [3] became the Gospel of those who, in his country or elsewhere, think decentralization to be, especially when resting on traditions, the ideal form of government.

This typically Spanish ideal of government was not without influence on the organization of Brazil during the union of Spain and Portugal. For instance, the system of vice-royalties with captaincies gravitating about them found a counterpart in the division of Brazil into two or three great states in opposition to the more plainly centralizing tendency in the Lisbon government.[3]

This theoretical centralization in Brazil did not affect, as we have seen, the extreme particularism which in practice served as a counterpoise or a corrective, exactly as, in matters of legislation, the lack of laws and general rules forming a definite plan of administration, was supplied by a multitude of special decrees and royal orders, which together formed the colonial *corpus juris*. We find on the subject in the work of the Belgian scholars, Lannoy and Van der Linden, a very happy passage based on the writings of an exceedingly able Portuguese author of administrative law, Coelho da Rocha [4]. This passage finds, moreover, a remote but not less valuable confirmation through the testimony of a book contemporaneous with the most brilliant period of Portuguese colonial expansion. This book is called *The Practical Soldier,* and is the work of Diego do Conto, the historian [5]. The Belgian author's page is the following:

"The institutions in the Portuguese colonies were mostly copied from those of the metropolis, without being, however, adapted to their new destination. Administrative organization never proceeded according to a uniform plan: it was determined by the march of events. The duties of

---

[2] This fact is clearly brought out by H. Van der Linden, *op. cit.* p. 253 *et seq.*

[3] It was only later on that Portugal saw fit to sever Para-Maranhão from Brazil proper, and in this case a number of special reasons were operative, *e. g.,* the vastness of the dominion conquered, the distance of these regions from the seat of the central authority, and finally the difficulties of navigation along the northern coast in a southern direction.

the many officials, their hierarchy and relations of service, were not stipulated by laws or general rules, but by a mass of special decrees, some appointing functionaries for the places, others dealing with the solution of a transitory difficulty or the suppression of some abuse. Often the adjustment of the different pieces of the administrative machinery worked of itself, as a result of habit or routine, sometimes in accordance with the designs of the central government, other times against them.

"If the Portuguese Kings since the reign of John II (1481-95) had their lawyers who gave to the laws of the Kingdom the interpretation most suitable to the interests of the crown, the colonial governors also had their own legal authorities, who furnished the texts with the meaning most favorable to the power of the chiefs who respectively employed them. It certainly is not an easy task to describe this administrative machinery, even when one knows the text of the laws and decrees which have organized it, which is not always the case; but it is still more difficult to explain their real working. It is frequently impossible to distinguish with certainty the laws that were applied from those which were not applied, or which were not applied as they ought to have been, and it is not without difficulty that we are enabled to define with precision the duties of the several authorities" [6].

These comments remind me of what was already said of us Ibero-Latin people, that we were in need of but one law—one which should put into execution all the existing ones. Such opinion appears naturally exaggerated in its gratuitous generalization, but if it be true that the application amongst us has not always corresponded to the intention; I mean, if often the ideal was not exactly followed in practice, we must bear in mind that the continuous effort towards a same direction finally reaches the end and accomplishes the *desideratum* as it was formulated. This is just the spectacle which Spanish-Portuguese America is affording, with her eyes turned towards a high and conspicuous mission in the history of mankind.

In such an earnest desire Latin America is helped by tradition, and you have already seen how much tradition is contained in our past. Confining ourselves, however, to the special subject of today's lecture, we must own that Spain was more coherent than Portugal in her constitutional orientation, for while she had her immense colonial empire divided into several administrative groups, separated and isolated, she allowed the tree of municipal freedom to grow and receive better care. On the contrary, in the Portuguese possessions, especially in Brazil, such liberties were occasionally assailed and destroyed.

This greater predilection for municipal freedom was but natural in the classic land of the *fueros,* although, as we have seen, when the municipal institution—an atavic expression of the Roman moral inheritance, peculiar to Iberian political life in the period immediately following the Christian reconquest of the Peninsula—was transported to the New World, the kingdoms organized in the Old World were already undergoing the crisis of centralization which was to go on increasing up to the storm of the French Revolution.

As a result, nevertheless, of colonial conditions, chief among which was that of distance from the metropolis, a system of checks and balances had to be formed, the key of which was represented by the division of powers, as was the case long afterwards with your wise constitution. So, the Spanish viceroys, direct and not always scrupulous representatives of the royal power—I do not mean that some of those viceroys did not greatly distinguish themselves by their spirit of equity and progress—could see standing before their thrones, as a counterpoise to their authority, the royal *audiencias* [7]. These august bodies joined to their judicial attributions a political character, since they exercised a supervision over the behavior of the Executive. Hence these courts assumed in a certain way the rôle normally played by the legislative branch of the government in those societies possessing self-government. Or looked at from another standpoint the *audiencias* contained in germ the function of the supreme court as it exists in your own country.

The tree, once transplanted, spread its roots in the soil of the three Americas. I do not refer to North, Central, and South America, but to English, Spanish, and Portuguese America. Federative union was the capital work of your first statesmen. The Brazilian Empire also sketched it, after having, by an effort of centralization, contrary to historical traditions, saved the political unity of a country homogeneous through its race and its culture. It was finally a federative union that the city of Caracas proposed to the other Colombian towns when it proclaimed its municipal autonomy in 1810, a year before the declaration of the independence of the country.

Such union, converted into a great American confederation, was the solution pointed out since 1790 by the precursor Miranda and reiterated in 1809 by the *Cabildos* of Buenos Ayres and Caracas as the best way to oppose Napoleon's policy of universal absorption. You well know that the execution of such a policy in the Iberian Peninsula gave the signal for the Spanish-American rebellion and was the starting point of the movement for the organization of the neo-Spanish nationalities of the New World.

We find a last trace of the Spanish administrative system by groups in de Aranda's [8] famous plan, the farthest-reaching one that was ever conceived by an European statesman regarding transatlantic colonies. According to this plan, which anticipated and surpassed modern British conception on relations between metropolis and colonies, Cuba, Porto-Rico, and a portion of South America to be determined later, were to remain under the immediate rule of the Spanish crown as possessions enjoying a limited autonomy, something like Jamaica or Guiana of today. All of the remaining Spanish-American colonies were to be divided into three large kingdoms or dominions—New Spain (Mexico), Terrafirma (New Granada), and Peru, which were to be granted to Spanish Infantes. The independence of these new kingdoms was to be conditioned only by the recognition of the Spanish King or Emperor, as suzerain, and the promise on the part of the Infantes to wed in the future only Spanish princesses.

The elder Pitt conceived a somewhat similar plan, when, in 1762, he was led to realize, on your refusal to join the British efforts in the war against France, that the hour for the emancipation of the English colonies in America was close at hand. In order to avoid a complete separation the great statesman conceived a sort of trans-Atlantic confederation. Canada, then conquered, would form the apanage of an English prince as an independent monarchy, while the remaining British possessions would be transformed into kingdoms, parts of a great Anglo-American league.

The motives which led Count de Aranda to advance his famous proposal of 1783 are well known. He desired to solve permanently the problem of the future relations between a metropolis which was losing in authority, and colonies which were gaining in strength, because he foresaw the puissance of your country, and desired to protect Spanish America from an absorption that seemed to him otherwise unavoidable. You will recall that this project was launched just at the conclusion of your Revolutionary War, in which France and Spain had been your allies against England. It is significant that on this occasion the minister of Charles III prophesied that Florida—just recovered to Spain from England—as well as New Spain or Mexico, would eventually be annexed by the United States.

The Spanish statesman was convinced that the United States would in the end dominate the great American empire at their door and he used to say that it would become impossible for Spain to avoid such an eventuality, as she could not think of opposing a powerful nation established on the same continent. We may say he guessed the Monroe Doctrine in its second meaning at least, as in the first it did not include any alliance with Latin American possessions revolted against their metropolis. Thus, Jefferson, when living in France as minister, in 1787, dampened the juvenile enthusiasm of the Brazilian student Maia, who, speaking on behalf of some vague, faraway conspirators, insisted on some help from the United States in favor of the liberty of his fatherland; and Monroe, as Secretary of State, pointed out that the obligations of neutrality would not permit any interference in the struggle between Spain and her revolted colonies [9].

Such, however, was not the attitude of France. Napoleon not only evinced an active interest in the political emancipation of Spanish America but even decided to lend active support to the revolutionists. And it was only the fall of the Empire, the agony of which began precisely in 1812 with the failure of the Russian campaign, which prevented a French contingent from associating with the Colombian troops in the Wars of Independence. It would have been a curious sight, that of English and French soldiers fighting under the same flag in the New World—the part taken by the British Legion in the decisive Battle of Carabobo [10] is well known—when in Europe both countries were such bitter foes.

Like Napoleon's intervention in the Spanish American Wars of Independence, the American monarchies fancied by Aranda never passed beyond the stage of a mere project. And yet it cannot be gainsaid that the establishment of these trans-Atlantic kingdoms, with their promise of peace and stability, was sincerely desired by not a few of those who subsequently became partisans of complete independence. That the timely foundation of such monarchies would have spared the former colonies of Spain much disorder and anarchy may be inferred from a study of the political evolution of Portuguese America. Imperial Brazil was indeed a model of order with progress, as soon as the country adjusted itself to the political mould which the federalist democrats had accepted as a temporary resource, and tried to destroy immediately after the separation from the mother country—an enterprise in which they were in the end unsuccessful [11].

The indirect influence of the United States upon the growing nationalities of Latin America clearly appears at this point. If the only existing autonomous government in the New World has assumed a republican form, corresponding to the model preached by ethnologists and doctrinaires and by the exalted partisans of action, it was but natural to see its example followed by the other nations of the continent, once the colonial dependence became a thing of the past. Brazil was not then in a position to exert a contrary influence. Her civil pacification was far from being a reality, and the beginning of the Empire was but the transfer of the seat of a monarchy from an European Kingdom to an American possession, in consequence of a number of very special circumstances. Yet the monarchical idea, reënforced and strengthened by its realization in Brazil—the best argument in favor of our Empire was the preservation intact of its imposing territorial extension—exerted a larger influence than is generally believed. A forerunner in a new and attractive field of historical investigation, the Venezuelan scholar Señor Carlos Villanueva, has recently published in Paris, on the subject of monarchical influence in America, a series of interesting books based on diplomatic papers found in European archives. The first two have respectively the titles of "Bolívar and San Martin" and "Ferdinand VII and the new States," and they are both published under the general title of "Monarchy in America" [12].

The subject is a vast one even when we consider only the period of the Wars of Independence with its spontaneous attempts to establish royalties in the New World. Such a survey would of course exclude the well known episode of Maximilian's empire, an event which must be considered rather as the result of a foreign imposition, or at least an attempt to apply to conditions in America a purely European political expedient. We may, however, be sure that Napoeon III would never have conceived the design of the empire of 1864, if he had not listened to the entreaties of the conservative and clerical elements in Mexico, alarmed at the bloody and sordid anarchy which masqueraded under the name of a republic.

The influence which the monarchical idea exerted in Spanish America in the second decade of the nineteenth century is seen in the anomalous situation which had developed in what is now the Argentine Republic. The Buenos Aires revolutionists, even the members of the Tucuman Congress had already considered the monarchical solution at the best calculated to spare the country the indiscipline of passions and the horrors of civil war. If a Spanish Infante, if Doña Carlota Joaquina, Princess Regent living then in Rio de Janeiro, had appeared at the Rio de la Plata, an acclamation would have been the immediate consequence and a delirium of enthusiasm would have followed.

In Venezuela, the other Spanish-American focus of irradiation of the feeling of Independence, aristocratic ideas prevailed against the monarchical ones, not because the republican form of government constituted the definite aspiration of an ignorant population, or even the ideal of the majority of the assembly which represented colonial intellectuality, but— simply because there was nobody to whom the crown might be offered.[4]

[4] This idea is admirably brought out by Señor Villanueva in his work La Monarquia en America, t. II, primera parte, *passim*.

As candidates for Spanish American thrones, Spanish Infantes counted indeed in their behalf considerations of race, customs, religion and affinities. Their political opportunity, however, had vanished, and such happy and logical conclusion of the political crises opened for the Spanish New World had ceased to be possible since a Bonaparte had taken the place of the legitimate sovereign on the throne of the metropolis. Such usurpation had shaken to its foundations the prestige of the royal Castilian house in the eyes of populations whose dynastic loyalty partook very much of the nature of hothouse plants.

There were even to be found monarchical enthusiasts who later broached the chimerical project of placing this same Joseph Bonaparte, the ex-king of Spain, at the head of a Mexican monarchy similar to that of Iturbide, or even ruler over a kingdom embracing the Rio de la Plata region. Obviously nothing could come of such fantastic plans. To understand how they could ever have been entertained we must bear in mind that, after Napoleon's fall, Joseph Bonaparte had come to live in the United States as a private citizen under the name of Count de Survilliers. The above-mentioned Venezuelan historian refers to such projects, which were a result of Bonapartist dreams, having as sole basis of reality the evasion of Napoleon from St. Helena. All these plans were foredoomed to failure, since England was mistress of the seas, and had therefore their execution at her mercy. England was even opposed to any scheme looking to the foundation of national, I mean, traditional dynasties in the old Spanish colonies, and the restoration of the Bourbons did not alter her views on the matter, as she was more pleased to deal with republics watched by her cabinets and protected by her fleets, than with monarchies allied to royal houses in Europe. A single exception was made in the case of the House of Braganza, on account of the Anglo-Portuguese alliance, a true protectorate of the stronger nation over the weaker one.

The British government of the time had established on her own behalf a kind of Monroe doctrine in reference to Latin America. England was the necessary intermediary between Portugal and Brazil and she was also the political godmother of the new Spanish-American republics. Mention of the Monroe Doctrine is the more suitable on this occasion as it was particularly inspired in Washington at that time by Canning—the same Canning whose ambition was the tutorship of a New World, which he so proudly proclaimed to have called to an international existence in order to reëstablish the balance of the Old. His best justification was that, after Napoleon's fall and Europe's pacification, Independent America had found in London her most valuable if not her only support against the Holy Alliance, formed with reactionary designs and hostile to the British liberal feeling.

It is an undeniable historical truth that the emancipation of Latin America was performed without any positive help from the United States: platonic sympathy or love is not, unfortunately, enough in such cases, and I even venture to say, in any case. On the contrary, England's support assumed a material shape: it was not precisely represented by troops—although some distinguished British officers, as Admiral Cochrane [13] and General Miller [14], were to be found in the revolutionary ranks, where no American commander was ever seen—but consisted in diplomatic, financial, and even military and naval facilities.

I am very well aware that the United States was not then the great power of our present time, and that she had just been again at war with her old metropolis, and could not but hesitate to defy absolutist Europe by extending tangible protection to Spanish America before reaching a diplomatic understanding with England. On the other side, I do not mean to say that the proceedings of the British government were dictated by reasons of pure social altruism, of mere international philanthropy—where would you find such principles flourishing in political environments?—but the truth is that things happened that way.

Rivalry between France and England fills up many centuries of modern European history—not to speak of the history of the Middle Ages—and British devotion to Spanish American rebels corresponds in a certain sense to one more feature of that rivalry. The war of Spanish Succession, provoked by the ascension of Louis XVIII's grandson to the throne wherefrom the shadow of the last king of the Austrian dynasty had vanished, has already been justly called by historical writers an economic war, and it is certain that, when associating her arms to Archduke Charles' fortune, England specially aimed at preventing the economic, much more than the political union of those two nations, divided until then by the Pyrenees, and now destined to be both ruled by princes of the Bourbon house.

The French colonial empire had not yet experienced the enormous losses of India, Canada, and Louisiana, and for England it was of vital moment to oppose naval French supremacy both in the Atlantic and the Pacific and above all in the Mediterranean—a supremacy which would be, even under an exclusive form, the sure sequel of an intimate alliance with Spain. Soon after, however, at the peace of Utrecht which followed the war of the Spanish Succession, Spain had to renounce her ambition to be any longer a maritime power in the Mediterranean, as she was compelled to surrender to England Gibraltar and Minorca. France, however, continued under a spell of colonial prosperity, for she did not have to abandon Canada or India before 1763, and Louisiana, ceded to Spain in 1762, was again in the possession of France from 1800 to 1804.

The names of Lafayette and Rochambeau will recall to you the support France gave to your Independence in revenge for the mutilations she suffered in her over-sea possessions through the loss of Canada and India. And it is a well known fact that Napoleon did not alienate to Jefferson a large part of your present West before trying, in Egypt and Syria, on the Mississippi and in the Caribbean Sea, to rebuild the former French colonial empire, causing the hated British supremacy to bleed to death on the faraway oceans as well as on the continent of Europe. Trafalgar destroyed such hopes, but the British government stood nevertheless on her guard, and did not conceal her fear of the revival of her colonial rival, when a Napoleon took in Madrid, the place of the Bourbons.

So the support of England, indirect, if you wish, but nevertheless important, brought in such emergency to Spanish America, had a double aspect.[5] In so far as it was dictated by a fear of France this support was political in character, as it was designed to check the plans of Napoleon and anticipate possible French expansion in the New World. As regards Spain, the aid accorded the struggling colonies was due primarily to economic motives, or it was the desire of England to convert into legal traffic with the new states the smuggling which for a long time had taken place to the detriment of the old metropolis. It is significant that commerce even used to increase after each of the wars that both nations sustained during the eighteenth century and through which the power of the Spanish imperial mantle was gradually wearing out.

We must acknowledge that you did not have in the United States the same reasons as did England and France for granting us your help. Let us hasten to add that the new American States, on their part, did not neglect the economic opportunities suddenly opened to them as a result of the new relations with Europe created by the Wars of Independence. The distinguished Colombian author Perez Triana says in the last volume of the *Cambridge Modern History* that Latin America's official debt to Europe—I mean the loans guaranteed by the governments of the respective countries, amounts to five hundred millions sterling, and that the

---
[5] Portuguese America need not be considered in this connection, as Portugal was at this time under the complete control of England.

double of this sum must be reckoned for the capital invested in private affairs—mines, agricultural experiments, industries, shipping companies, banks and so forth.

Considering such an intimacy of interests between Latin America and England and the consequent harmony of views, it seems natural that a monarchical feeling, derived from British constitutionalism, might have permeated the first essays of autonomous organization of Latin America, in opposition to your republican suggestion. Its action was in fact perceptible, the more so as England had been a constant model for the partisans of monarchy. Yet this influence was neutralized by the efforts of a few leaders who had rather shown a decided taste for democracy. The minds of these republican enthusiasts were inspired by French philosophy and still more by all the events which since 1787 had been occurring in Europe with striking rapidity.

The same thing was, in fine, happening in the New World as in the Old: both here and there the two tendencies, the aristocratic and the democratic, the monarchical and the republican, stood face to face. Hence the same time that in Mexico the King of Spain himself was proclaimed Emperor and for want of an Infante who might be placed at the head of the autonomous Kingdom of New Spain, her government assumed the form of Iturbide's military and spurious monarchy, a similar constitutional crisis developed in the extreme South of the Southern continent.

The erection of a throne on the territory of La Plata engaged, after 1815, the best activity of Argentine diplomacy, as it has already been the greatest preoccupation of the men who in 1810 had undertaken the responsibilities of independent government. The romantic tendency went so far in this direction that it was seriously proposed to galvanize into life the theocratic despotism of the Incas, decked out in all the gala trappings of liberalism. Somebody even thought of harmonizing dynasties, nations, and races through the wedding of the last descendant of Atahualpa and Tupac Amaru to one of the Portuguese princesses, daughters of John VI and Queen Carlota Joaquina [15].

These picturesque absurdities, which already announced the Indianism [16] so characteristic of the next literary period should not blind us to the fact that this monarchical ideal had captivated some of the greatest minds of South America. San Martin himself, the glorious soldier who gave Chile her freedom and, in his desire to deprive Spain of her last South American redoubt, even penetrated into Peru, had been as early as 1812 a fervid partisan of a monarchical form of government for the new states he had helped to bring into being. Moreover, Belgrano [17], Rivadavia [18], Pueyrredon [19], and all those who belonged to the Supreme Dictator's party fully shared San Martin's views, but owing to circumstances foreign to their wishes, their choice wavered amongst a whole gallery of princes, passing from the Duke of Orleans, the future King of the French, Louis Philippe, to the Duke of Lucca, an Italian Bourbon.

The name of the last candidate aroused an interest entirely disproportionate to his historic importance. Even the British Parliament was deeply agitated at rumors that this inconspicuous Italian princeling might secure a majority of the votes of those Argentine statesmen bent on importing a foreign monarch. Behind the Duke of Lucca the English descried the French Foreign Office, guided by Richelieu or Chateaubriand, developing such an intrigue in a sense favorable to French dynastic interests. At this juncture such interests were identical with those of Spain, and were coupled with political aims opposed to England [20]. Only the statesmen of the *Restoration* failed to appraise at their true value the stupidity and obstinacy of Ferdinand VII, one of the monarchs who have least deserved the title of king,—a ruler who would justify any republic. He it was indeed who, in his intellectual dullness, only rendered more evident by his innate perfidy, chiefly ignored the New World's events and showed himself most hostile to an agreement. Foreign diplomatists, amongst whom figured the French plenipotentiary, describe him as indifferent to the loss of his absolutist rights.

A crisis had arrived in the reign of Ferdinand VII when a policy of shuffling and tergiversation was absolutely fatal. Events in the New World had been moving with kaleidoscopic rapidity. The victory of Carabobo had set Venezuela free; Cochrane and San Martin had reached Peru and begun her conquest, the Peruvian royalists having themselves called La Serna [21] to the palace of the viceroy Pezuela [22]; the viceroy of Mexico, Apodaca [23], had abdicated and his successor, O'Donoju [24] had felt himself compelled by a general rebellion to take refuge in Vera Cruz; the Mexican representatives to the Constitutional Cortes had made an eloquent appeal to Spanish liberals, pointing out how it was still possible to keep a good intelligence and even a certain union through the foundation of American monarchies. But the incapable sovereign, intent only on the preservation of his despotic power, refused to recognize the changed situation that had arisen in America. Any compromise in which his absolute rights might suffer a curtailment was repugnant to him and in his dilemma he thought only of imploring the intervention of the Holy

Alliance as a supreme measure of dynastic and public salvation, identifying both in a case where one was in no wise synonymous with the other. So unhappy an attitude gave to French royalty the opportunity of winning for the Duke de Angoûlème's expedition the laurels of Trocadero [25], and to Chateaubriand the pretext for obtaining at Verona the right of intervention and for restoring by himself the plan of the Spanish American monarchies. The king of Spain was consequently the principal obstacle to the realization of those projects of a general importance for the New World, since even Bolívar himself, at a given moment, was ready to accept monarchy as the best solution for the crisis. It is to be noted however that the *Libertador* remained inflexible in his antagonism to Spanish princes and in his insistence that if thrones were to be erected in Spanish America they should be occupied only by natives.

Bolívar also evinced a lasting abhorrence to all these monarchs of a local color or taste, especially after the miserable Napoleonic parody given by Mexico through her general Iturbide, who with the help of clergy, nobility and people, imitated the 18th Brumaire and even improved on it—as it was the Mexican Congress that under the gun's pressure went so far as to vote the proclamation of the empire of Augustine I—carrying the parody up to the *Sacre* with all the ceremonial adopted at Notre Dame for the *Emperor* [26].

The simile ought to stop here, as this exotic court lacked in its pageant, to soften the contrast with public distress, the splendor of military conquest. Yet even the return from Elbe found its counterpart in Mexico. After the deposition and banishment of Iturbide by Santa Anna—an easy task as the emperor displayed faint hearted resistance—the poor ex-sovereign determined to overcome the results of his pusillanimity and inertia by a return from Europe to the New World. He was arrested on landing at Mexico, however, and shot three days later.

You will see that the spectacle was of a nature to kindle the republican sentiments of Bolívar to whom, like Caesar, the crown was thrice offered. As to San Martin, if he had not left the struggle in 1824, disgusted and grieved, that precedent would have confirmed in his mind the belief that only a constitutional monarchy, *with an European prince at its its head,* could spare the independent New World the flood of blood and infamy in which it nearly disappeared.

San Martin calculated the power of this tide of lawlessness and insubordination by the conspiracies which his officers themselves plotted against him, specially after the arrival in the capital of Peru, when the troops that had freed Chile plunged in those new pleasures of Capua, and lost the best of their warlike nerve. And it was precisely the disappointment of not being able to persuade Bolívar to share his royalist conception—as the monarchical *feeling* was common to both—that chiefly induced San Martin to desert public life. In the famous interview of Guayaquil [27], in July 1822, the two systems—the monarchical and the oligarchic—met and collided. Bolívar's ambition, quite natural in a man full of imagination, of reserving for himself the glory of definitely liberating Peru and achieving the wars of Independence, dashed against the logical wish of San Martin's reflexive mind, not to forsake, until the end had come, a campaign which he had initiated. As it always happens in such cases, disinterestedness gave way to ambition—ambition for honors, let us say, not for personal gains, as these lower motives had not yet subdued the minds of the *Libertadores* of South American countries. Bolívar found the field too narrow for two South American glories, both of them seeking after the palms of immortality: Napoleon would have thought exactly the same way. San Martin did not want for an egotistical reason to delay the conclusion of a political enterprise which possessed a vital interest for a whole continent. So Washington would have acted.

This historical parallel suggests itself in such a way, it occurs so easily, that you will not be surprised to learn that it has often been made and often repeated. We shall soon present it once more as it explains in a certain way the evolution, apparently contradictory, of Spanish America. Meanwhile I have mentioned such a comparison because it facilitates the understanding of what happened in that famous interview at Guayaquil—an event which has proved to be an inexhaustible source for varied and ofttimes conflicting commentaries on the part of the historians of the period.

A document of a considerable value on the subject has even been recently published: no less than the dispatch addressed, on July 29th, 1822, by Bolívar's general secretary to the Secretary of State for the Foreign Affairs of Colombia [28]. In this dispatch it is said that San Martin insisted that an invitation be extended to some European prince and that Bolívar, though simulating indifference for the form of government of each State taken as a unit, opposed himself decidedly to the introduction of a heterogeneous element in the national mass (*sic*). Such indifference was however so much the less sincere as Bolívar's dream of federation, expressed during the interview, could only rest on similarity of constitutional systems. It would have been quite impossible to associate monarchies and republics at a time when their mutual antagonism appears most clearly and the principles represented by both forms of government were violently arrayed against each other.

Yet it is conceivable that a democratic federation might have at its head an *imperator*. Republican Rome lasted nominally, as a political faction, on into Imperial Rome, in the same way as the French Revolution lasted on into the Napoleonic Empire. There was apparently no break in the continuity and besides, the essential thing was the stability of the system, much more than the European character of the dynasty, which could only have served to stimulate rivalries amongst the Old World's powers.

In fact, Colombia's minister plenipotentiary in London—let us give him this title by anticipation—had written to Bolívar in 1820, after a conversation with Lord Castlereagh, that Spanish-American independence would be acknowledged by all powers as soon as an hereditary executive power had been established, under any denomination whatever, in the new republics [29]. Europe wanted more than anything else the recognition of the nationalities which she had helped to establish; the monarchical idea represented, even more than a question of principle, a question of opportunism, as it always happens with every political question under its practical aspect.

The application of a remedy, considered the only one possible for healing the disorder in which the Spanish American republics had fallen in such a short period of life, could not therefore be regarded as unadvisable in this domain, and we must not then be surprised at the statement of such well informed historians as Señor Carlos A. Villanueva that "laying bare the mind, the heart, the intimate feelings of Bolívar, we will find that he always thought of a native monarchy, disguised or declared, under England's protectorate, as the exclusive way of assuring his work and saving his glory. He had never conceived"—such are the textual words of a writer who has deeply studied his subject—"a democratic republic, as he judged impossible its consolidation."

At the critical moment the great man's ambition lacked the requisite decision, or if you prefer, the impudence which would have led him to place on his own head, crowned with laurels, the royal diadem which had been offered to him and which he had sought for, perhaps only to allow himself the impressive gesture of refusal after some grandiloquent phrases about liberty. Perhaps in the consummation of such a plan he was checked by what I may call doctrinaire remorse. If for such reason his memory became dearer to the republican moralist, his work decreased in the eyes of mankind.

Great Colombia was shattered into fragments in the pursuit of that mirage of democratic solidarity. Her leaders forgot that the foundation of one or more Spanish-American monarchies, similar to ours, to which Brazil was indebted, first for her union, and then for her pacification, would have spared the Christian civilization of the nineteenth century many bloody and grotesque pages. If my own country can boast of her history during the last century, if she can relate it to other countries with some pride, she owes it above all to the liberal influence of imperial institutions. Historical truth must not be immolated to prejudices, even if such prejudices be democratic or derive their sanction from foreign suggestion.

Indeed it is enough to read letters and memoirs of the Era of the Wars of Independence to be convinced that the ideas of unlimited equality and liberty did not find unanimous approval in colonial circles. There was, in fact, a large proportion of minds that might be called moderate. This condition of affairs need evoke no surprise when we recall that there was a certain proportion of the partisans of Independence who were either self-educated or had derived their liberal ideas from Spanish sources. Among these men the horrors of the French Revolution could not but excite a repulsion and feelings of revolt, for the influence to which they had been subjected emanated, as was just suggested, from Spain rather than from France, although a reflection could never stand in competition with the original shining light of French intellectuality.

Spanish ideas displayed during the eighteenth century some visible tendency towards poltical and social reforms. I have already mentioned the progressive ideas of Charles III, and it may not be amiss to remind you that the most remarkable men of Spanish-American Independence— Miranda, San Martin, Bolívar, O'Higgins [30], Belgrano—lived all of them more or less in Spain. There they came in touch with those liberal aspirations with which the educated minds of the Peninsula were permeated. And these same aspirations were carried back to America by the colonists, in germ, so to speak. Here under more favorable conditions they not only gave theoretical and superior expression to local discontent but with further development directly paved the way for emancipation.

Hence emancipation was not a spontaneous or sudden revelation: it had its causes, its precedents, in a word its traditions. Spanish historians wisely establish a distinction between rebellions of protest against acts or measures of governors or Companies—mutinies without a preconceived plan, true *straw fires*,[6] as they are called in Portuguese and in French—and revolts guided or inspired by the idea of autonomy. These scholars find this second kind of revolt in several risings of the eighteenth century in Peru, Chile and Venezuela, even in insurrections of Indians, negroes and mulattoes [31].

Those historians, amongst whom I will mention Professor Rafael Altamira [32], do not also conceal that in official papers, such as the reports of viceroys and others, there are to be discovered sure and unsuspected evidence of the discontent existing among the cultivated natives due to the reason already pointed out—that the Spaniards from the metropolis enjoyed, so to speak, all official positions. The *Visitador* of New Spain, Galvez,—"visitador" was the name given to the royal commissioner charged of an inquiry into the administration of a certain viceroy or captain-general, about whom complaints happened to be presented to the sovereign—wrote in 1761 that the natives, I mean the *criollos*, had condensed their grievances into a set formula: "Spaniards not only don't allow us to share the government of our country, but they carry away all our money" [33]. Mexicans even requested Charles III to grant them admission to public functions.

If at that time there did not yet exist in the colonies that definite patriotic feeling so conspicuous after the Wars of Liberation, there were not wanting evidences of what we might term a local patriotism. In fact this sentiment was so strong that it was the support given by England to the revolutionary attempt of Miranda in 1806 that chiefly contributed to the indifference shown by the dominating local class in Venezuela regarding such ill-fated separatist movements. In reality, however, the apprehensions of the Venezuelans were groundless. In supporting Miranda, England was intent only in aiding the colonies to sever their relations with the metropolis. In other words she was not seeking territorial aggrandizement as was the case with the British expedition against Buenos Aires in that same year, 1806 [34].

Such exclusivism is thoroughly characteristic of the Spanish national feeling: amongst you, on the contrary, French help was welcome, as if cosmopolitanism began even then to foretell its own advent. It is true that you could not harbor fears of foreign supremacy, and that any help of that kind contained a sure guarantee of success of a noble enterprise, already fully launched. For your own Revolution, long before the proffer of French or Spanish aid, was already the direct expression of a

---

[6] Or, "feux de paille," "fogo de palha."

national conscience, or, to be more strictly historical, of a union of collective consciences, from States that had reached the age of emancipation.

In Latin America this spiritual evolution synchronized with, and in a large measure resulted from, the political crisis engendered in Europe. Yet it would be an error to minimize the influence of events which occurred in South America on the eve of political emancipation. For instance the defeat of the English and consequent reconquest of Buenos Aires by the city militia, which until then only served as a theme of mockery for the European Spaniards established in the colonies, had a repercussion throughout the colonial empire. Such events inspired courage in the local population deserted by their viceroy and so led to victory by Liniers' [35] daring mind, with the self-confidence which had so far been strange to them. Liniers practically proved—and his demonstration could not but produce extraordinary effects—that the armed population was capable of defending itself against any foe, domestic or foreign, even though this foe might dispose of every means for the success of his attempt.

In this current of local patriotism, whose existence had been hardly suspected, was merged another current of a more truly national character, determined by the struggle which the mother country was sustaining against French dominion. The result was that latent colonial aspirations, apparently discordant, but alike in essence, emerged, so to speak, to the surface of national consciousness. Thus old atavistic instincts, stimulated by the Bourbon abdication—for it was generally denied to the King the right of disposing in that way of the fidelity of his American subjects—came to combine with feelings of personal loyalty to this same unfortunate monarch, violently deprived of his crown. The party of independence chiefly displayed its ability in disassociating itself from the Cadiz Regency [36] through the declaration of a direct dependency from the crown, that is, the strictly personal tie which bound colonies to their sovereign. On this basis, identical in all sections of Spanish America, the various colonies without any concerted action set out to secure a complete autonomy. Such autonomy was tantamount to separation from Spain, for when the first colonial risings occurred, the belief was general that Ferdinand VII would never again occupy his throne. On the strength of the doctrine proclaimed by the colonists and consecrated by several jurists, the colonial empire refused to acknowledge the authority of the boards or "Juntas" which called themselves delegations of the Spanish nation: the suzerainty of the nation, as such, was by right null and void over America, which was an exclusive apanage of the monarch, and not a national property.

LECTURE IV.

Representative types in the struggle for the independence of the New World.—The Mexican curate Hidalgo and the Latin American clergy, partisans of national independence.—The Brazilian priests in the revolution, in the Constituent Assembly and in the government.—Temporary union of the aristocratic, religious and popular elements.—The creole royalty of Iturbide and the imperialistic jacobinism of Bolívar.—The conservative and the revolutionary elements in the new political societies.—José Bonifacio, Dom Pedro and Brazilian emancipation.—Bolívar's political psychology and its historical parallel with that of San Martin.—Their double sketch in the light of sociology, by F. Garcia Calderon.—Their antagonistic temperaments and different education.—Federation applied, and the international ideal of Bolívar: solidarity, mediation, arbitration and territorial integrity.—The pact of Panamá and the abstention of the United States.—Bolívar's nationalism, his generosity.—Nativism of the subsequent *libertadores*, more in harmony with the environment.—Melancholy destiny of the superior men of the Independence and of their patriotic work.—Advent of the anarchic element, premature political decadence, and dawn of regeneration.

IN the Latin American countries as in yours, the idea of Independence was not embodied in men of plebeian origin but in the aristocracy, a circumstance that really corresponds to the existing moral and social status of the nobility and common people. This fact remains true even if we take into consideration the differences that existed between the many colonial communities and their varying degrees of development. Such a circumstance proves once more the truth of the aphorism that the government always belongs in point of fact to the minorities, though in theory to the majorities. It proves after all that the emancipation of the New World was much more a political than a social problem: a carefully worked out result of a preconceived intellectual plan—in which, to be sure, there were evidences of a determined will—rather than the instinctive consequence of a rebellion engendered by spite and hate. These tendencies, on the one hand social, on the other political, are both to be found in such capital events of the history of our countries, although the first one in a much smaller proportion, so as to vanish into the other. The French Revolution, for instance, was both one thing and the other, and finished by becoming more social than political, by aiming at equality after the proclamation of liberty whether or not based on fraternity.

It is true that in Mexico we see as a leader of the party for independence, when it was first initiated, a most typical commoner, the priest Hidalgo [1], of whom Morelos [2], another priest, was only a second edition more within the reach of the popular element. This appearance, however, of the clergy in the battlefields was in such cases due to nativistic or patriotic, rather than to social reasons, as the lower clergy in Latin America was all composed of natives, and some of them even were halfcaste. The church made it a point never to accept the prejudice of color. On the other side, the high clergy, the ecclesiastical hierarchy, was European by birth and in mind.

When the crisis for the separation took place, naturally the national clergy almost without exception embraced the new cause as a matter of patriotism, and as they represented to a great extent, if not almost entirely, the cultivated element, it was also quite natural for them to find themselves at the head of the movement, consequently in the number of those who had really to fight. Thus we find the explanation to the curious fact of a liberal, republican, and revolutionary Roman-Catholic clergy in the New World, in perfect contrast to what happened in Europe, where it was for the most part reactionary, dynastic, and absolutist.

In Spanish America, where the idea of democracy had at last identified itself generally with that of independence, the contrast became for that reason less extraordinary than in Brazil, though it was equally noticeable here. The establishment in 1808 of the Portuguese court in Rio de Janeiro, with the benefits emanating from it, worked as a stimulant for the monarchical feeling, and I have already mentioned how, after the departure of the King to Lisbon, the presence of the Heir Apparent as regent supplied a center to which might converge the efforts of all partisans of the national emancipation. Despite this fact, the Revolution of 1817—which for months maintained a republican form of government at Pernambuco and even appealed to you for a direct positive help—was, so to say, a revolution of priests. In fact, a number of its leaders, many of its propagandists, and not a few of its martyrs, belonged to the clergy. No European liberals, no French revolutionists ever felt their hearts throb with more enthusiasm for the cause of liberty, than those clergymen who paid with their lives on the gibbet for the democratic aspiration of their souls [3].

The Constituent Assembly, which the first Emperor of Brazil had to dissolve because it pretended, under the disguise of ultra-liberalism, to carry too far its oligarchical designs, contained a strong proportion of priests, and this faction was precisely the most advanced in political matters. Fascinated by the lively French of the *Encyclopédie,* those priests had forgotten the tiresome Latin of their breviaries, and their religious gowns only served to enhance their resemblance to the Conscript Fathers of the French Republic. Brazil even counted as regent, during the minority of her second Emperor, a priest, Feijo [4], and he was the most radical, as well as the most energetic of the men who succeeded at the head of the State in the course of that historical period, which has been happily compared by a remarkable political writer, the late Joaquim Nabuco [5]—who died as ambassador from Brazil to the United States—to a true test of the republican system. In spite of his clerical character—slightly tinged with heterodoxy, to be sure, as he strongly opposed, for instance, ecclesiastic celibacy—Feijo did not hesitate when in power to dismiss the army invaded by the worst militarist virus, to arouse the civic zeal among the citizens, trusting to them the defense of public order, to suppress anarchy and to enforce justice.

Priests of this kind did not have much time left for their religious occupations; they surely neglected their spiritual mission and I even admit that their lives were not positively edifying, as most of their useful time was taken up by political duties and whatever remained was only too short for the charms of a family, for the great majority of the clergy had abandoned a life of celibacy. It was only later on, in the Roman movement represented by the *Syllabus* [6] that the ultramontane spirit pervaded the Brazilian clergy. This new influence was on the whole distinctly salutary in character; it did not in the least affect the traditional patriotism of the clergy while it produced wholesome effects in their morality. Moreover it tended to eliminate the religious element, especially as represented by ecclesiastical ministers, from the struggles of the various political parties for power—struggles not infrequently accompanied by violence and bloodshed [7].

Father Hidalgo [8], the monastic leader of the Mexican rebellion of 1810, a kind of tribune of the people who had deserted the pulpit for the forum was not only an active but a cultivated mind, brought up in the ideas of the French philosophers of the eighteenth century, initiated in the physiocratic doctrine, a partisan of the political and social reform capable of transforming the old societies. Hence he was far from being a vulgar agitator, a plebeian energumen: only he could not help having as his first revolutionary troops a band of a few peasants displaying the standard of the Virgin of Guadalupe, uttering threats of death against the Spaniards and cheering the king. They tried in this way to associate the equality of rights—a thing utterly unknown to them—with dynastic fidelity, of which they nourished a vague suspicion.

From that time on we may see Latin-American revolutions undertaken through the spirit of plunder, though cloaked with the principles of liberalism. If Bolívar or San Martin, or any other like these, possessed the true and superior notion of fatherland and liberty, those who were grouped around them were nothing else than herdsmen to whose savage instincts the devil of destruction made the strongest appeal. I do not mean to imply that they did not understand the elementary freedoms —freedom of movement, or right of assembly, for instance. In order to give a concrete feature to his appeal to liberty and enlist the support of the popular elements, the Mexican curate of Dolores did not fail to abolish at once both slavery and the Indian tribute. The episcopal anathemas which Hidalgo called upon himself for this reason were invalidated by other ecclesiastical authorities, on his seditious march forward.

The civil struggle between royalists and rebels quickly and easily assumed the ferocious character which distinguished it through all Spanish America, although in Mexico, as well as in Venezuela and Buenos Aires, personalities from the higher classes did not delay in joining the popular movement towards independence. Some were driven by a certain plan of the King—Ferdinand VII—to emigrate to New Spain, exactly as King John VI of Portugal had emigrated with his court to the Brazils; others were determined by questions of class or rather class interests, postponed or menaced. We find on these last, in the very recent and excellent book of the Venezuelan historian Carlos Villanueva— *Ferdinand VII and the New States*—a work which constitutes the second of the series I have already mentioned, with the general title of *Monarchy in America*, the following information which greatly helps us to understand the particular development of the movement of Independence: "The reëstablishment of the Spanish Constitution of 1812 by the liberal revolution of Cadiz in 1820 (the so-called rising of Riego) produced in Mexico a deep sensation, especially among the clergy, as that organic law had abolished all church privileges. Seeing that the new constitutional system of the metropolis would not grant them better conditions than those afforded by the Mexican revolutionists in the event of the latter's victory, the priests and monks thought finally to come to an alliance with the rebels in order to try and save some of their prerogatives. Accordingly they began to support the new local revolution, which took on a theocratical character, more definite than that assumed at the time of Father Hidalgo's rising at Dolores; now it was the high clergy that held the leadership of the party of emancipation, a party which found in the events occurring in the Peninsula a fit opportunity for their aims" [9].

Let us say that in Mexico, as well as in the other Spanish colonies of America, the party of Independence, after the first enthusiasms and the first victories, had known—as it also happened with you—a period of defeats and discouragement, before recovering its strength and winning a definite triumph. The colonial royalty of Ferdinand VII, which fascinated many by its strange feature and seemed logical to many others on account of the Spanish anarchy, an anarchy that even called for foreign intervention, was planned to be autonomous and restricted, that is, the legitimate King of absolutist Spain would become the constitutional sovereign of free Mexico. This is enough to allow us to reckon the advance already taken by the idea of emancipation, fatally destined to a full execution. We must add that such a monarchical solution of the crisis of separation bound to the local revolutionary cause the territorial aristocracy and the creole officers, besides other native elements which in the beginning had nourished justified fears of the Indian soldiery of the rebel priest Hidalgo.

It was after all the monarchical solution which prevailed with the accession to power of Iturbide, transformed by his imperial acclamation into Augustin I. His military talents had become famous through his alleged prowess in the struggle against the rebels, and his social position was an element of prestige, as he belonged to a rich family. Thus you see that also in Mexico, where the revolution at its inception was invested with both popular and religious elements, the movement ended by obeying the guidance of the superior elements of the population.

This characteristic of a conscious orientation weighed at least as much as the plebeian fetishism for anything that smacked of royalty in favor of the acceptance on the part of many colonials of the idea of the establishment of one or more Spanish-American thrones. We have already seen how, on the contrary, the *Libertador* Bolívar was a strong antagonist of such ideas. He himself was noble and once rich, but he had immolated caste advantages and privileges of fortune upon the great political ideal which inflamed him, and in which we discern so strongly united a civil and aristocratic jacobinism, that may only find its model in Greece, and a military and democratic imperialism, of a true Roman origin. We must never forget that the sad destiny of the creole royalty of Iturbide must have surely and strongly contributed to keep Bolívar's mind aloof from the temptation of the crown, which more than once was offered to him by his admirers and his flatterers. Hence he contributed more than anybody else to maintain far from America the scions of the Spanish dynasty who might be tempted to encircle their brows with American diadems. The well-known Spanish writer Labra [10] judiciously divides the American population of the Spanish possessions of the time into three classes: the first, devoted to a radical autonomy, composed of the intellectual élite and the lower clergy, all natives; the second, attached to the pure colonial system, to the despotic government of the metropolis, composed of the Spanish authorities, the higher clergy, likewise of Spanish birth, and the possessors of privileges; the third comprising the merchants, industrials, and planters, and numbering as many Europeans as colonials. This last class fully appreciated all the wrongs which their interests suffered from an imperfect local administration and an unhappy economic policy, but at the same time feared the party excesses certain to follow in the wake of suddenly acquired liberties. Hence, this third class practically represented a conservative ballast, and was little inclined to follow, without thinking, the rather limited revolutionary element. Señor Perez Triana says in the article in the *Cambridge Modern History* to which reference has already been made, that a Spanish victory at Ayacucho [11], in 1824, when the movement of Independence had already become concrete, general, and consolidated, would have still meant the reconquest by Spain of her lost possessions. Such a remark coming from an eminent South American writer may well excuse and justify the tenacity displayed by the metropolis in not recognizing the republics issued from her.

The proportion of Spain's followers was indeed large until the very last moment amongst the nationals of those new countries, and the majority of the colonial populations remained during the struggle neutral and indifferent, ready to go over to the side of victory in the same way—so says Señor Perez Triana—as the waters follow the declivity of the soil. The local, or creole aristocracy generally belonged to the moderate group, and it only felt obliged to exaggerate its liberalism, which had been noticed by Humboldt, when the European element accentuated its reactionary tendency. Those noblemen by birth went then as far as to join the agitators who at that time preferred to attract the colored population, opening before these unknown horizons, and involuntarily awakening those instincts of destruction ever slumbering beneath the surface.

The priests who played such a considerable rôle both in the Mexican and in the Pernambuco Revolutions, the Hidalgos and the Morelos, the Ribeiros [12] and the Romas [13] belonged to the class of those agitators and we also reckon amongst them, both because his career helps explain the mental evolution just discussed and especially because of his particular idiosyncracies, the most renowned historical personality of South America—Don Simon Bolívar.

This name is familiar and, I willingly fancy, also dear to you, as well as that of his great rival San Martin: rival I mean in the admiration and gratitude of their countrymen that is, of all Spanish-Americans, as both of them aimed at the same high and noble purpose, which was the freedom of a whole colonial world aspiring to its independence. When fate made them meet and set in opposition if not their methods, their own ideals, and behind these, their personalities, San Martin, as we have seen, yielded the field and definitely retired from the political stage allowing Bolívar to reap the laurels of Junin [14].

Venezuela and Buenos Aires were in Spanish America, or at least in South America—as the Mexican rising was apart, though contemporaneous—the two centers of irradiation of the idea of Independence, personified in those two leaders who in Peru, the chief center of resistance, came to dash one against the other in their double and simultaneous projection. The board of *vecinos notables,* or notable citizens, comprising the *Cabildo abierto,* that is, open meeting of August 14, 1806, which obliged the inept Viceroy of Buenos Aires, Sobremonte, to transfer the military command to Jaques Liniers and the civil authority to the "Audiencia," had been in the Latin New World the first true essay of the representative system and of political autonomy [15]. On the other side of the continent the resistance of the captain-general of Venezuela to the action of the local board organized to direct the affairs of the captaincy, independently of the Supreme Central Board of Seville, which had assumed royal attributions, was one of the immediate signs of the prolonged civil war which for so many years drenched Spanish America with blood [16].

In Brazil the principal effort would tend, not towards separation, but towards the maintenance of a cohesion still conventional, like that of the "State of Brazil," coupled with the union of the "Para-Maranhão State" [17]. The result would be a whole imposing by its size, attained through the integration of elements disproportionate amongst themselves and badly assembled. Yet this same disproportion, the result of administrative action, was more apparent than real. The language, the religion, a common past and the character of its individual settlers—whose general feature absorbed the other insignificant European contributions to the race of the invaders—gave the country a decided and remarkable uniformity. There are few countries besides yours, which offer such a homogeneity of moral aspects as Brazil.

The task of uniting the political elements in one patriotic purpose belonged in Brazil to José Bonifacio de Andrada e Silva, a learned mineralogist, an eloquent academician and a thoroughbred statesmen, who found in the Regent, Dom Pedro, the fittest instrument for the execution of such a work. We may even say that he was predestined to exercise a decisive influence in the history of Brazil at this crisis. The importance accorded by the future emperor to superior principles of administration, the prestige which Dom Pedro enjoyed as the representative of institutions prized by all patriotic Brazilians, the personal qualities of intelligence and bravery for which the young ruler was conspicuous—all facilitated and perhaps rendered possible the great achievements of José Bonifacio [18].

The exclusion in itself of the dominion of the metropolis did not cost a big effort. Resistance indeed amounted to none, a fact which endowed the independence of Portuguese America with a character both logical and productive. At the same time there was necessarily lacking the romantic note assumed by the Revolution of Spanish America, thanks to the prolonged struggle which surrounded with an everlasting glory the personalities of Bolívar and San Martin.

At this point we find ourselves compelled, for a better comprehension of the subject, to have recourse to a historical parallel, in spite of the banality and vulgarity of such a literary process. Yet such parallels may be more than mere theoretical devices and may even, as will presently appear, partake of the quality of scientific precision. By a natural disposition easy to understand and even as a result of a point of honor, although historical justice must always be supreme and exclusive, Venezuelans and Argentines respectively praise with the utmost enthusiasm Bolívar and San Martin, at the same time trying, in the antagonism of their feelings, to lessen the merits of one or the other of the two heroes. And as there is no human personality without fault, it is not difficult for them to perpetuate their discussions on the matter.

So, obeying the instinct of impartiality, I address myself to a Peruvian writer, son of that land of pre-Columbian traditions, of colonial traditions and of heroic traditions during the cycle of emancipation; a land which was, as we have seen, the bulwark of loyalist resistance and the field of concentration for the troops which came down victorious from the Pichincha and for those which equally victorious came up from Maypu, all anxious to secure the freedom of the Spanish New World [19]. Fortunately the writer whom I speak of, Francisco Garcia Calderon [20], is a master of sociology and one of the most balanced and thoughtful minds of Spanish America at the present time. You will judge better of his capacity by the parallel he once established between those two illustrious men whom Hellenic antiquity would have transformed into demi-gods and who would have been classified by our contemporary Nietzche under the epithet of *Supermen*: "This American movement is concentrated in two great names: Bolívar and San Martin. In their psychological differences we are to find the image of the two revolutionary tendencies: in one the boisterous rupture with the past, imitation of the French Revolution and of the American Federation, equality to the prejudice of liberty; in the other the conservative mind within the revolution, new ideals soothed by traditionalism, respect and amplification of the monarchical ideal, liberty above equality. Those two forces, as exemplified in Bolívar, the man of the North, and San Martin, the man of the South, combined to repudiate the past, but were arrayed against each other in every thing that concerned the affirmation and building up of the future.

"In cast of mind they presented marked contrasts, Bolívar being ambitious and egoistic, of a despotic disposition, although great and visionary in his egoism; San Martin being loyal, sensible, timid, dominated by traditions. A genial and generalizing mind, the psychological type of the creole, Bolívar was bound to become an egotist; as an utopian he wanted to organize everything, to govern everything, to adjust minds to the same inflexible mould; he possessed the illogical spirit of all the great builders. San Martin, devoted to monarchy, devoid of ambition, and destitute of a commanding temper, submitted himself, like the Greek statesman to ostracism and returned with his daughter, a pious and faithful Antigone, to the heart of the monarchical traditions of France [21].

"We discover, however, in their fatal clashing more than the opposition of two different types of mind: rather do we find the play of two historical forces, the acting of two methods of social construction. Bolívar imitates Napoleon and San Martin reminds us of Washington. They establish the principles of democracy according to different conceptions. Bolívar was to triumph by his genius, by the suggestion of a high and growing ambition, by the excesses even of his work, and with him came the turn of administrative centralization, of political instability, of exaggerated equality, of social confusion. Bolívar was more American than Napoleon was French; he followed the hereditary feelings of his race and suffered the action of the environment, but possessed the originality of genius. Only, in America, the dominating qualities of our Bonaparte seem to weaken: the marvellous fibre, the primitive vigor, the energy of the *condottiere* are not the same . . . Both pronounce the *fiat* in the chaos, disclaim ideology and are idealogues, by their symmetrical mind, by their system, by a kind of political catholicism. Passionately fond of unity they both desire the coördination of all things on a unitarian plan.

"Napoleon, more imperative, aims at the mastery of the Revolution over Europe by way of imposture and jacobinism; Bolívar looks for liberty in America through confederation, by means of the political solidarity of his race. They both establish democracy through the amplification of their own power, as they represent authority, rising above the ordinary level of human affairs. They resemble each other in the determination and vigor of their social action. The first one is a solitary carnivore, the big human specimen, a marvel of Nature; the second her only child, the last expression of her creative power." [1]

Taine marvellously described the integrity of the mental instrument in Napoleon, this strength which discovers unity amidst things heteroclitic and disseminated, this organic reconstruction of life in the dominating mind. Bolívar possesses a more analytic intelligence; in his unifying impetus he simplified things, and in spite of himself acted as an idealogue; his mind was rather critical than creative. He was the first to lend a direction to the revolutionary organization. His power was absolute to establish, to test, and to destroy. He governs people, distributes provinces, changes boundaries, founds Columbia, is absolute master of Peru, conceives a republic, Bolivia, to which he leaves his name; he aims at Roman unity and aspires to be the Caesar of a magnificent American centralization. The evolution of the American continent is but the reflection and realization of his thought: the military spirit, the influence of a strong personality, the complete creation of codes and constitutions, the nervous instability of collective movements, emanate from him.

San Martin is the emulator of Washington and like him aims at political objectivity; he knows how to extricate himself from the fatality of events. He gives his effort without imposing a rule and shows a tenacious and strong will, the sense of circumstances and of the progress of things. We find in him the spirit of moderation, the respect for the slow evolution of realities. A monarchist and a liberal, he wishes to interpret in a traditional sense the fatal movement of the Revolution. Like Washington he sees in "time and habit" the true foundations of social organization; he cherishes the same religious feeling for liberty, the same civic virtues, and the same puritanism. Before all else they are heroes of peace. Living in the same historical period, Bolívar and San Martin were destined to engage in the inevitable conflict, as they represented political systems based upon fundamentally different conceptions,

---

[1] "Le premier est un fauve solitaire, le grand specimen humain, une trouvaille de la nature; le deuxième est son fils unique, la dernière épreuve de l'effort créateur." Garcia Calderon, *Le Pérou contemporain*, p. 64.

the Latin *imperium* and the Saxon individualism. Such clashing reminds us of the differences which developed between Jefferson and Hamilton during the administration of Washington. Hamilton, the courageous founder of *The Federalist,* upholds traditions, accepts aristocracy and federalism and only fears, like San Martin, the devastating tide of democracy. Jefferson, more liberal than Bolívar, cherished an equal hatred of privilege and in a generous impulse wishes to exalt every autonomy.

Washington did not believe in definitive formulas. He looked for the conciliation of the two political ideals, accepting both unity and federative autonomy. His theories of government and of the state were neither exclusive nor intolerant; it was possible to rally to their support without any sacrifice of moral spontaneity. On the contrary, South America allowed a simple, uniform, and authoritative model to be imposed upon her without the complexity and variety of life.

The adaptation, which was necessarily to follow, of an abstract mould to concrete realities, was destined to fill the last century in the Latin-American world with an agitation often idle, but not always barren. In some respects it was even productive, for along with much material and moral misery it resulted in a certain degree of common and promising progress. I beg, however, to be allowed to carry a little further a parallel which singularly contributes to clear up that understanding of a subject hitherto enveloped in much obscurity.

If we look through the biography of the two *Libertadores,* we shall see that San Martin was since his very first youth brought up on military discipline. As a cadet in the Spanish army, he fought against the Moors, the French, the English, and the Portuguese, going from Oran to Rousillon, from Bailen to Tudela [22], from the Mediterranean shore to the Portuguese province of Alemtejo. Early initiated into the secret revolutionary societies, he became an active propagandist of the movement for Independence; at the same time his numerous campaigns endowed him with the ability of a military leader, incapable of far reaching war plans, but knowing well how to prepare for victory.

Bolívar was quite a different mind. Joining intuition to the military art, and improvisation to strategics, capable, however, of genial inspirations, he was consistently to play the part prepared for him by his reveries, combined with an extraordinary tenacity—which urged him on to great deeds,—and by his education as a man of the world, who had traveled extensively and could shine in society. San Martin was as prudent, steady and considerate, as Bolívar was garrulous, turbulent and audacious. In the former, all the faculties gravitated towards conscience; in the latter they were wont to fly on the wings of fancy and their colors acquired a variegated scale through a prism formed in its three faces by oratory, suggestion, political egoism, and the ideal of freedom. So, we may well understand that San Martin's influence increased after his proud retreat and the abnegation of his last years in a foreign country, and that Bolívar, nowadays a little forgotten, occupied a large place in the sympathy of his European contemporaries. His name was even popular in Ireland and Poland, countries fighting for their emancipation like his own. French liberals paid him the same admiration offered as a tribute to Napoleon and Washington, and fashion showed how popular he was by giving about 1820 his name—which it never lost—to a wide-brimmed hat of a decidedly inspiring aspect. Finally Carlyle, who never refused homage to heroes, called him a "genius whose history would be worth the ink employed in writing it, if only the Homer capable of such a task could be found."

The points of contact or, better said, the resemblances of genius between Napoleon and Bolívar are numerous and striking. Both possessed an imagination that was not only lively, but may even be called exalted. Bonaparte when in Egypt incited the courage of his soldiers at the same time that he gave expression to his own historical feeling by saying that "forty centuries were contemplating them from the top of the Pyramids." Bolívar wrote in an ecstacy from Chimborazo that he had reached the glacial region, where no human foot had been able to pollute the resplendent crown placed by Eternity on the lofty front of the dominator of the Andes: "I faint"—such are his words—"on touching with my head the vault of Heaven."

In both, however, imagination did not exclude a practical intelligence. Napoleon, the victor of Marengo and Austerlitz, was not only the author of the Concordat with Rome which gave satisfaction to the religious spirit of France, which had been suffering unjust persecution, but was also the compiler of the well known code of civil laws which assured the moral conquests of the French Revolution. Bolívar, the victor of Boyacá [23] and Junin [24], was also, as I have had already the opportunity of reminding you, the one who inspired in this international domain in which all Americans try to meet and to read a good understanding regarding such free principles as territorial integrity and compulsory arbitration. The first of these was, when it was proclaimed, a principle exceedingly conservative, as it attributed to each new sovereign State the same extension it had as a colony. So it gave the old administrative delimitations a prerogative of political boundary and—*uti possidetis juris*

—it granted the political unities, created at that time without corresponding precisely to the economic unities, not only the territories occupied *de facto* but also these possessed *de jure*.[2] If unfortunately such principles did not abolish throughout our double continent every war of conquest, at least it substituted at the worst moment, when the new Spanish nationalities were being organized, the prestige of tradition and the rules of Right for the use of brutal strength.

According to Bolívar's plan, a Congress of plenipotentiaries or American amphictyons was to give obligatory sanction to the sentences deciding the pleas between the delegations of the new governments. In the words of the *Libertador* it was "to initiate the system of guarantees which, in peace as well as in war, ought to be the shield of our destinies, and to consolidate the power of the great political corporation in the exercise of its sublime authority which was bound to lead our governments, maintain through its influence the uniformity of our principles, and appease by its single name the fury of our tempests."

The pact concluded at Panama on July 15, 1825, unfortunately without the complete approval of independent America, included some articles which contained those very principles of international law that nowadays have represented the greatest desideratum as well as the greatest obstacle for those who in the last Peace Conferences have fought on their behalf. I am going to read for you three such articles, so that you may see how the noble efforts of your President in favor of a wider scheme of arbitration have their precedents in our New World.

Article XVI, for instance, dealt with the principle of recourse to mediation: "The contracting parties engage themselves, and make thereto a solemn compromise, to settle in a friendly way all differences that presently exist or may arise among them. In case the agreement should fail, the powers in controversy will present their cases, in preference to any violent solution and with the design of reaching conciliation, to the consideration of the assembly, whose decision will however not be obligatory, if said powers have not previously decided so." Such a condition was of a nature to guarantee the full sovereignty of every one of the contracting parties, a sovereignty which many feared to see sacrificed to the convention for compulsory arbitration.

Article XXI would have endowed the Monroe Doctrine, already formulated at that time, with that wide character—I mean the full responsibility of the compounding parties—which it does not yet possess: "The contracting parties engage themselves, and make thereto a solemn

[2] A. Alvarez, *Le Droit International Américain.* (Paris, 1910.)

compromise, to maintain and defend the integrity of their respective territories, opposing themselves efficaciously to any attempt of occupation without the corresponding authorization and dependency of the governments to whom such territories belong in domain and property. They otherwise engage themselves to gather for such purpose, if necessary, their forces and resources."

Article XXII, notwithstanding its equity, has not yet been able to win a general approval in the recent Pan-American Conferences which have taken place in the last twenty-five years. It was conceived in these terms: "The contracting parties will reciprocally guarantee the integrity of their territories as soon as, by virtue of the special conventions celebrated between them, they will have determined and deliminated their respective boundaries, the maintenance of which will then be placed under the protection of the Confederation" [25].

The adhesion of the United States failed to assure the reality of the pact of Panama and I think that you are acquainted with the reasons of such an obstruction. There existed at that time in your South, which in public affairs wielded a greater influence than the North, a feeling of violent hostility to anything tending towards the abolition of slavery. This sentiment was stronger than the aversion to a military alliance of the double continent superimposed on that commercial alliance which is now so eagerly sought. The same feeling existed in Brazil and precisely one of the topics to be discussed at Panama was the one referred to. On the part of your public men there was also to be found a reluctance to allow the freedom of Cuba and Porto Rico—a freedom secured only in our own day—to become a matter of general discussion.

In spite of his Americanism—he was indeed the first one to give expression to the feeling which received much later the name of Pan-Americanism—Bolívar never ceased to cultivate the spirit of nationalism. San Martin's military novitiate in Europe had rendered his mind somewhat a stranger to his native country. Bolívar, on the contrary, always belonged essentially to his fatherland, and this feature added to his intense power of magnetism contributed in no small degree to enhance his prestige.

When deserted by his rivals, repudiated by the nation he had created, vowed to ostracism, Bolívar did not feel the courage to abandon the shore of his beloved country: he expired at Santa Marta, tortured by many grievances. Meanwhile San Martin, without renouncing his love of country, preferred exile when he realized that his rule was thought too heavy.

The greatest fault with Miranda in the eyes of the leaders of the

Wars of Independence was that he seemed a stranger to them. The one day favorite of Catharine of Russia, the soldier of the Revolution in two worlds, had finally lost every touch with his nation, and his melancholy fate did not excite great compassion when Bolívar delivered him over to the Spaniards. This decision of the national leader was as inhuman as that of Napoleon ordering the Duke d'Enghien to be shot in the moats of Vincennes, although Bolívar explained his action by saying that he had seen in Miranda almost a traitor owing to the latter's readiness to receive overtures from the enemy and to renounce the perils of the struggle [26].

Yet Bolívar, like Napoleon, was capable of high generosity, not only of a private nature, as his refusal of every donation voted by Congress as a reward for his deeds, but of a public character. "I leave to your sovereign decision," Bolívar declared in 1819 before the Congress of Angostura, where the organization of Great Colombia was sketched, "the reform or recall of all my laws and decrees: but I beseech you to confirm absolute liberty of the slaves, as I would implore for my life and the existence of the Republic." To the Congress of Cucuta, which consolidated that political unison, he addressed in 1821 from Valencia a message in which he said: "The sons of the slaves who will henceforward be born in Colombia must be free, because these beings belong only to God and to their parents, and neither God nor their parents want them unhappy."

Other *libertadores* more closely in touch with their environment might succeed Bolívar, but they did not exhibit the same noble feelings. The fratricide wars which followed political emancipation left in their wake material devastation, social confusion, and moral degradation; the crimes perpetrated called for an expiation, and the high altruistic conceptions of Bolívar were not in harmony with the surrounding society which sought to accomplish them. Bolívar himself had no illusions regarding the task of political adaptation which he noticed around him. "Generally speaking," so runs his program of Carthagena, written in 1812, "our countrymen are not yet in a condition adequately to appreciate their new rights and privileges, as they are lacking in the political virtues which ought to characterize the true republican: such virtues cannot be acquired under absolute governments, when the rights and duties of the citizens are practically unknown."

This is why the excellent principles of international law proclaimed by Bolívar are only now truly put into practice and constitute a common ideal, after having received new vigor from the political society in which they were first formulated as well as from the communities to which they were addressed. "A century later the ideals of the *Libertador* subsist," so wrote recently, at the occasion of the centenary of the Independence, one of Bolívar's admirers, the Colombian statesman Francisco José Urrutia[8]: "but, as is natural, they have undergone the influence of a more advanced civilization, in which the capital preoccupation of the defence of the territory and of the sovereignty in its several manifestations is accompanied by the great aspirations of justice, of peace, and of progress which nowadays animate the society of nations."

This same realization of the progress already accomplished is the keynote of an eloquent speech by another South American statesman, the well-known Argentine, Drago [27], whose name is associated with that great doctrine of international law destined to triumph, and the germ of which is to be found in Bolívar's antagonism to the use of force in international contests. Such were his words: "South America begins to emerge from this unprejudiced period of childhood which only cared for problems claiming for immediate solutions. . . . All force and all tendencies of civilization concur to couple patriotism, without diminishing its vitality, with a feeling of benevolent tolerance capable of suppressing miserable jealousy and petty rivalries and suspicions, in order to draw humanity together, independent of racial conception, all of it working for the common welfare. So, the old ideal of Christianity must once more become our inspiration and our teaching in order that the political boundaries of the American continent may serve, not as barriers separating peoples, but as the counterparts lending greater solidity of the total structure, or the water-tight divisions which in the well-built ships confine the invasion of water in the moment of danger to prevent a shipwreck."

Any idea that creates proselytes, engenders at the same time suffering. Every noble cause counts its martyrs, as well as its apostles. The abolition of slavery counted amongst you John Brown: amongst us the foremost men of the Wars of Independence did, however, suffer what yours did not suffer in the corresponding struggle. And in summarizing the causes of this apparent anomaly, I repeat with pleasure in my own words a quotation from a United States historian. These causes were in fine "the stability of the political machinery, the spirit of the multitudes, the religion of respect toward liberators, the practical good sense, the inadequacy of the surroundings to the slanders of demagogy, the lack of fuel for the revolutionary fires, the want of taste for the rash and violent reforms."

The specific absence of some of those qualities well explains the very

---

[8] *El ideal internacional de Bolívar.* (Quito, 1911.)

different spectacle offered in its development by the Latin society of the New World. The above-mentioned Colombian writer, Urrutia, wrote on the subject a melancholy page, which I cannot resist the temptation of reading to you—even because the chief scope of these lectures is to give you, as much as the shortness of time and the competence of the lecturer permits—an idea not only of the mind of that Latin-American society, but of the literary shape taken by the traditional expression of its intellectuality: "How dark, how tragic the destiny of the liberators of peoples in South America! Our soul shrinks with pain when, looking towards the past, we see the faith of precursors of that work followed by the liberators themselves, all touched by the hand of an inexorable fate. The Venezuelan, Miranda, ends his life, as fruitful as unfortunate, in a miserable dungeon. The first liberators in Bogotá, Quito and La Paz, ascend the scaffold, as does Hidalgo in Mexico. Rivadavia [28] dies in exile, and Belgrano [29] in obscurity and poverty. O'Higgins [30] did not avoid proscription: he also drank to the dregs the bitter cup of disloyalty and ingratitude. The same happened to San Martin, who suffered with stoic fortitude, on foreign soil, the privations and sorrows of his last years. Sucre [31], the virtuous and magnanimous Sucre, fell a victim to a treacherous hand on the mountains of Berruecos. Bolivar, with murderous daggers risen against his heart, his soul a prey to mortal anguish, and his body overcome by fatigue and illness, goes in search of his grave on the shores of the Caribbean Sea: 'Yes, the grave . . . that is all my countrymen reserve for me, but I forgive them. . . .' Washington was allowed to expire blessing his work; Bolívar, tortured by scepticism, had to doubt his own; immortality smiled to the first before reaching the tomb; the mystery of the unknown surrounded the second and poisoned his painful agony."

In Brazil neither Dom Pedro I [32] nor José Bonifacio [33] escaped a like unmerciful fate. The so-called Patriarch of Independence learned the way of exile as soon as his imperial master had violently dissolved a Constituent Assembly which seemed to aspire to the rôle of a Convention, for it was in this assembly that the great statesman of the first days of the Empire represented, with his two distinguished brothers, the liberal vanguard within the monarchical form of government. Even during the regency, although it was a parliamentary government, José Bonifacio was the object of unjust suspicions provoked by his reconciliation with the Emperor, who had abdicated in 1830. He was even compelled to give up the tutorship of the infant monarch—the future Dom Pedro II—who had been entrusted to him by his father Dom Pedro I, the same sovereign who had proclaimed the national emancipation of Brazil, and who now was forced to leave the country in ostracism. Why such a divorce between the superior representatives of the national organization and the nationalities founded by them? The fact is, that when the lower elements demanded the price of their coöperation in the common work of political liberation, they did not meet with the necessary resistance from the higher elements, whose ardor had cooled down after the struggle, and who did not know on which foundations to build during the peace which followed the confusion of war. Rising against the earlier conservative and aristocratic oligarchies and subduing them, the elements composing these new anarchical strata rendered everything anarchic.

Bolívar had the foreboding of this sad destiny of his work, because prevision, an essential virtue for the politician, counted among his high gifts as a statesman and projected its lights over the noble and vast plans in which his mind was always absorbed. It was even this feature that made him in a certain sense so superior to San Martin, whose genius was that of a soldier rather than a statesman.[4]

Bolívar uttered in 1822 this prophesy: "Neither our generation, nor the one which is to follow, will see the lustre of the Republic we are establishing. I consider America as a chrysalis. . . . There will be in the end a new fusion of all races, which will give birth to the homogeneity of the people." As regards Brazil, it has already been said that the freedom we enjoyed under the Empire and which contrasted so much with the spectacle offered by the other Latin-American countries—since those which progressed beyond the chrysalis state did so only in the latter part of the nineteenth century—was rather granted by the monarchy than conferred by the citizens. Hence Brazil was a stranger to the enjoyment of that effort of adaptation in its fullness, which comes as the result of her own activity. For this kind of historic evolution, there was substituted the introduction into her body of a foreign though generous blood—if we may call foreign an institution which was indeed after all a national expression, although brought forth by a concurrence of circumstances.

In any case, Imperial Brazil constituted a model of liberty and peace for Latin America and furnished at least a real image of civilization, reflected from the throne, at the time when Spanish American Societies struggled in disorder and savagery. This period of anarchy was ushered

---
[4] Cf. e. g., San Martin's remarkable passage of the Southern Andes in 1817, comparable only to the similar deed of Bolívar in the Northern Andes—both of them reported by the military writers of our day as far superior to the passage of the Alps by Hannibal in antiquity and by Napoleon in modern times.

in by the appearance of leaders like Paez [34], in Venezuela, and Quiroga [35], in the region of the River Plate—men who emerged from the ranks of the illiterate populace and hence were better understood and cherished by their uncultivated countrymen.

The processes of transformation spread and became general in all those false democracies sprung from the Spanish colonial disaggregation, and neither the nobles nor the doctrinaires, of the kind of Monagas [36] or Alberdi [37], could oppose effective resistance to these upstart leaders just mentioned. The type of the chief crystallized itself, meanwhile, in the well known *general*, dominating a fascinated and unconscious multitude in which prevailed, regarding social matters, a communist instinct, and regarding political matters, a demagogic tendency. Now, demagogy, like communism, is not a system which can resist the strong pressure of an individual energy combined with firm temper and well served by circumstances.

The temper of the metal has nothing to do with the use of the arm. The celebrated Argentine tyrant Rosas [38], who, although deprived of education, belonged to a good family, rested his ferocious power on the mutinous and bloodthirsty mob. His was one of the most miserable and sinister episodes of the struggle extending through all the former Spanish Empire between the new *Goths*—a nickname given to the old supporters of the metropolis—who were the conservatives, attached to their political interests founded upon social hierarchy, and the revolutionists, ambitious of power and contending for it in the name of liberty, in order to acquire the pleasures and benefits which could be in this way obtained.

In such an onslaught of the inferior elements of those political societies, the tradition of probity was lost,—a tradition which had distinguished the first generation and still distinguished Rosas, insensible and cruel but not dishonest though he was. Bolívar came out a beggar from a struggle in which he had entered rich, and maintained himself noble to the end. San Martin suffered real privations at Boulogne. José Bonifacio, when in the cabinet, was at a loss for his expenses, because a pickpocket relieved him of his monthly salary, which he had received and carried to the theater; his brother Martin, secretary of the Treasury, peremptorily refused to give execution to the imperial order granting a new payment of the amount lost, but divided with the victim his own salary. The tyranny of Francia [39] in Paraguay, absorbing, crushing as it was, remained nevertheless zealously and absolutely honest.

The period of peculation and administrative immorality was initiated with the worst tyranny, the tyranny of the mob, which in such cases is so easily ruled by envy and hatred. All regular authority having disappeared, the feeling of authority itself having vanished, the anarchy which was to pervert all public morality took its place, and from such anarchy there came only temporary relief in crises of despotism and prepotency.

So, the federalist bond that should have fastened the administrative units in a vigorous and splendid political chain, degenerated through all republican Latin America into a round of Satrapies, where everything was dependent on the whims and abuses of the chief satellites of the greater chief. Such corruption brought on the ruin of all that representative system, depriving both the executive and legislative branches of their legal titles and, in the incisive word of a late Brazilian political writer, making any rebellions against those constitutional powers as legitimate or at least as illegitimate as they themselves were.

On the other side, political sophistication incited satraps to defend to the utmost local autonomy, as such autonomy implied their own omnipotence. No wonder that, conceived and applied in this way, federalism has given birth to civil wars, homeopathic republics, and a hospital of nationalities counterfeit after the image and resemblance of the United States—so writes the above named publicist, who was an eminent jurist with a personal parliamentary tradition.[5]

The life of those countries was soiled and spoiled by a radical and in a certain sense hereditary vice, that of political activity without civic education. This vice renders oppositions seditious and governments arbitrary in our societies, establishing such deep contrast between the private manners of the citizens, open, pleasant, generous and tolerant, and their public manners, intransigent, violent, persecuting and even sanguinary.

There exists, however, exemption for this original sin. Through our continent, demoralized by the degradation of political habits, a consequence of the disfigurement of the noblest ideals by means of ignorance and greediness, a tendency toward moralization by labor and education has been progressively taking shape. Brazil cannot offer a proof as suggestive as other countries, of the incontestible results obtained in this direction, because her past of yesterday, under the monarchy, was worthy of being envied; but the Argentine Republic, for instance, is a living document, for it is not long since she contrived to free herself from the mire in which she had sunk, and to present before the world a comforting spectacle played by practical sense, professional education and industrious activity.

---

[5] Dr. A. Coelho Rodrigues, *Memoires sur l'union et la pacification de l'Amérique Latine et de l'Europe, addressés au XXIe Congrès universel de la Paix de 1912.*

LECTURE V

The work of neo-Latin emancipation and the Iberian-American element.—Andres Bello and Mariano Moreno, types of superior colonial intellects.—The books which San Martin and Bolívar read.—Critical sense of Bolívar.—The poem *Junin*, by Olmedo.—Constituent assemblies and constitutions.—The "Middle Ages" of the new Spanish-Portuguese World.—Its first intellectual currents.—The liberal ideas of the generation of the Independence and the part taken by the colonial representatives in the Cortes of Cadiz and Lisbon.—Character of the literature of the new countries.—Heroic poetry and the Indianist school.—The tradition of the mother-tongue among the neo-Spanish peoples.—The cult of the Past.—French influence in literature and politics.—The Eclecticism of Cousin and the Positivist training.—Effect of English and German philosophies.—European Idealism in America.—Science and mental speculation.—Traditionalism and Modernism.

THE possibility of a general insurrection of the Spanish possessions of America,—as general as if obeying a preconcerted compact, and based upon motives apparently as legitimate and, in any case, as well founded, as the noble repudiation of foreign usurpation which had taken place in the mother country,—is in itself an argument in favor of the colonization work, which, in her own image and likeness, Spain had undertaken across the sea. We see that the separation was followed by the political and social organization of a number of more or less progressive nations whose organization was excellent in theory but only indifferently efficacious in practice.

The work of the mother-country was a great work, even as that of her children turned out to be, for it may be said that Conquest and Emancipation rival each other in their power and far reaching influence. And if, as the distinguished Venezuelan, Angel Cesar Rivas, in his admirable address on the occasion of his entry into the Caracas Historical Academy, has well said, that if there is anything that serves to differentiate races into superior and inferior, it is unquestionably a capacity for accomplishing great social or political undertakings which have as their chief elements perseverance, energy, aptitude for self-control, and that combination of rules of procedure respected from earliest times as the basis of the aggregate of ethical conceptions which is called morality. The same statement was made by the illustrious Andres Bello [1] at a time when there was less cordiality between the mother-country and the over-sea off-shoots, than in these days, when we have just witnessed, at the celebration of Independence at Caracas, the kindred of Bolívar fraternizing with the descendants of General Morillo [2]. His declaration is the more noteworthy because Andres Bello was Venezuelan by birth, Chilian by adoption, American in heart and soul, the living exponent of the intellectual and moral identity of Spanish America.

This celebrated poet, grammarian, jurist and professor, wrote that a people thoroughly degraded and devoid of courageous sentiment never would have been capable of performing the great deeds that distinguished the campaigns of the patriots, the heroic acts of self-forgetfulness, the sacrifices of every kind whereby the different American sections won their political emancipation. "Every one who observes with philosophic eye the history of our struggle against the parent-land," writes Don Andres Bello, "will recognize without difficulty that what enabled us to conquer in it, was precisely the Iberian element. The officers and veteran legions of the trans-Atlantic Iberia were conquered and humiliated by the leaders and improvised armies of that other young Iberia, which, while abjuring the name, still preserved the indomitable spirit of the Old Spain in the defence of their homes."

Andres Bello is himself one of the best examples of the actual value of preparation, of which the educated colonial element gave proof at the period of the secession and political and social reconstruction of the new nationalities. Another notable example is found in Mariano Moreno [3], Secretary of the revolutionary Junta of Buenos Aires, who, in spite of his youth, for he was scarcely 32 years of age when he died, displayed a remarkable promptness, decision and clearness of vision especially in all that pertained to intellectual emancipation. This noble-minded Argentine defended liberty of thought as applied to the press, libraries, and schools in the following terms: "Let us for once be less partisan of our antiquated ideas; let there be less self-complacency; give free entrance to Truth and to the introduction of Light and Learning; let there be no repression of innocent liberty of thought upon subjects of universal interest; let us not believe that this can ever attack, with impunity, Merit and Virtue, because with these gifts themselves testifying in their own favor, and always having the people as their impartial judge, the writings of those who unworthily presume to attack them will cause their own destruction. Truth, as well as Virtue, holds within itself its most convincing defence; discussion and scrutiny only cause the splendor and glory of both to become all the more apparent; if restrictions are placed upon speech, the spirit will vegetate as does matter; and error, falsehood, selfish preoccupation, fanaticism and brutalization will constitute the watchword of the people and will cause their irrevocable decadence, ruin, and misery."

It might be said that we were listening to one of your earliest defenders of political liberties, to a Thomas Paine or Patrick Henry, with all their practical moderation joined to civic enthusiasm, rather than to one of the ardent disciples of the French Revolution, still less to a fanatic of the Convention. As a matter of fact, all the self-taught Latin-Americans —for in reality, that is what they were for the most part, as was also the case with many of the European thinkers of that period—had imbibed the French inspiration far more than your own.

We are ignorant of the books which formed the minds of many of the children of the Spanish-Colonial revolution, but our ignorance fortunately does not extend to the principal actors in the drama. We know that San Martin delighted in the military work of Guibert [4], the one to whom were addressed these burning epistles of Mlle. de Lespinasse, and that it was in the Manual of Epictetus that his soul sought the lessons of stoicism which made it invulnerable. As to Bolívar, the curiosity of his spirit divided itself among the utilitarian doctrines of Bentham, the subversive principles of French Encyclopaedists, the self-centered metaphysics of Helvetius, the scepticism of Hume, the melancholy and dangerous vagaries of Jean Jacques Rousseau, the ethics of Spinoza, the materialism of Holbach, the rationalism of Hobbes, and the wide and sure political vision of Montesquieu.

We are not surprised, in view of this wide culture, at the literary expression in which this great South American warrior and statesman knew how to clothe and was in the habit of clothing his thoughts and ideas. We are not even surprised by the critical sense evidenced by him in his delicious irony regarding the otherwise very beautiful pindaric poem of Olmedo [5], entitled "Junin," in which the beauties of versification redeem the affectations of style. I cannot resist the temptation of reading you a page of Bolívar's reply to his poet-friend, asking you to note that the letter is dated from Cuzco, the classic Inca Land of the Sun— the land of fable and story, as it is called in this letter, and that scarcely a year had passed since the battle of Ayacucho [6], which raised the Liberator to the pinnacle of Glory. Observe, notwithstanding, the gracious playfulness with which he addresses his bard:

"You explode . . . where there has not been the slightest discharge of a gun; you set fire to the earth with the sparks from the axle and wheels of a chariot of Achilles, which never rolled in Junin; you lay hold upon all the personages and make of me a Jupiter, of Sucre, a God Mars . . . We all have a divine or heroic spirit which shelters us with protecting wings like a guardian angel. You adapt us to your poetic and fantastic style, and in order to prolong in the land of poetry the fictions of the fable, you raise us with your false divinity (the divine father of the first Inca, Manco-Capac) as the eagle of Jupiter carried to the heavens the tortoise which it must needs let fall upon a rock where the poor thing broke its claws. In the same way you make us beings so sublime that you plunge us into the abyss of nothingness, drowning in an ocean of light the pale lustre of our not too transparent virtues. You thus reduce us to ashes, my dear friend, with the lightening of your Jupiter, the sword of your Mars, the sceptre of your Agamemnon, the lance of your Achilles, and the wisdom of your Ulysses. If I were not so good, and you were not so much of a poet, I would go so far as to think that you desired to make a parody on the Iliad with the heroes of our poor farce. But no; that I do not believe. You are a poet, and you know as well as did Bonaparte that there is only a step from the heroic to the ludicrous, and that Manolo and the Cid are brothers, although born from different fathers. An American will read your poem as a canto of Homer, and a Spaniard, as a canto of Boileau's *Hyssope*."[1]

This extract is sufficient to give you a clear idea of the capacity for intellectual activity of that generation of colonists; of their capacity for moral activity, of which none but a cultivated people would be susceptible, you can form an idea, remembering that it was so great as to cause the patriotic fervor manifested in the liberation of the New World of Columbus to be rightly regarded as equal to that manifested in the reconquering from the Moors of the Iberian Peninsula. Nor does a century—for that is the period passed since the dawn of Iberian Colonial emancipation—seem too long a time for a continent to reëstablish itself after such an upheaval.

It is evident that when one speaks of cultivated people and of patriotic fervor, reference is made to a restricted minority, whose worth it is given us to measure by the above-mentioned names of Bolívar and Andres Bello. This man of many-sided talent denounced, as a poet, the influence of the Didacticians of the eighteenth century in France, of whom Delille was the mouth-piece. As a jurist, it was he who proclaimed in South America the first principles of that law of nations which became one of the favorite fields for the intellectual activity of the societies which

---

[1] *Le Lutrin.*

there flourished and where they succeeded not only in introducing liberal ideas, but in attaining tangible results. Finally, as a philologist, he edited the best grammar of the Castilian language, which that other master of neo-Spanish philology, Rufino Cuervo [7], of Colombia, lately deceased, reëdited and modernized, amplifying it by his profound learning, both men revealing thereby a feature upon which I will touch later, that is, the devotion to the nation's past, manifesting itself through devotion to the national tongue.

The legislative assemblies that met here and there in different places of their sessions contain many praiseworthy documents of learning and may be regarded as unmistakable exponents of the colonial culture. Many of their members had never crossed the ocean; nevertheless, the reports of their sessions contain many praiseworthy documents of learning and ability, side by side with the inevitable childishness and ingenuousness of political inexperience.

In Venezuela, the minutes of the first Congress which proclaimed the separation, were republished the past year, from which we see that courage and confidence were not wanting in this Constituent Assembly. Without the Congress of Tucuman [8], the Argentine Confederation would have fallen entirely to pieces, completely justifying the saying of Bolívar that in the Spanish American lands a great monarchy would have been difficult, and a great republic impossible. In Brazil, the Assembly of 1823 [9], although dissolved as seditious and, in fact, very jealous of her liberty of action and very suspicious of imperial loyalty, comes near to being, for those who today scan the records impartially, a model legislative assembly, not only for its tried patriotism, but also because of the clearness of its political vision.

The project of the Constitution which it drew up served to shape that which had been elaborated by the first State council of the Empire, sanctioned by the sovereign, and accepted by the municipal chambers of the country, after it had been expurgated, of course, of everything that resembled democratic excrescences, but preserving alive all the liberal spirit which shone so brightly at that time, the flame of which was only fanned into greater brightness by the reaction which sought to extinguish it. This liberal spirit finds marked expression in the religious tolerance which throughout Latin America took the place of a fanaticism that had become traditional, although this was not so complete or blind, as many have tried to make us believe. The following admirable words are Bolívar's: "In a political constitution no religious creed should be prescribed. . . . Religion is the law of conscience. All law pertaining to

Religion annuls Conscience, because in making duty a necessity, all merit is taken away from Faith, which is the basis of religion."

It is curious to observe that in the assemblies in which the organic laws of independent Latin America were modeled, the predominant moral influence was not so much yours, as it was directly French. These laws were among the finest triumphs of the Encyclopedists. Emancipation of thought, the forerunner of political emancipation, was developed under the influence of these reformers, and their work—namely, the naturalist theories of Rousseau, the impassioned doctrines of Diderot, the negativist synthesis of d'Alembert—was that which first changed the guides of the movement towards separation, so that they became strangers to their own fellow citizens, among whom the rule was intellectual, quite as much as administrative, subserviency.

I have already had occasion to speak of this lack of correspondence with environment. This was the first of the difficulties against which the Latin-American reformers had to struggle when they tried to free themselves from the trammels of a century of mental and moral stagnation, as the third colonial century has been termed, following, as it did, a first age of struggle and lack of discipline, and a second age especially notable for its colonizing activity.

Francisco Garcia Calderon aptly styled all this period the "American Middle Ages," and indeed it vividly recalls to our minds that historical age, a kind of a crust under which intense fermentation was seething. To use another figure, it was as if beneath the slimy surface of a body of water were circulating currents unseen and unnoted by the ordinary observer, yet possessing sufficient force to transform the apparent calm into a boisterous sea. Then we see huge waves arising—the waves of Humanism and Reform—and despite Catholic and Absolutist reaction, the agitation does not grow more calm, but instead bursts into the storm of 1789, the effect of which was felt in Latin America as the reflex flow of a distant, violent tempest.

Across the seas, as in the Iberian Peninsula, the defence of Catholicism and even of Absolutism, had been confided to that special institution called the Inquisition, which did not actually exist in Portuguese America; those guilty of being Jews and heretics were transported to the Kingdom of Portugal for punishment. Scholasticism brooded over education, while erudition undertook to satisfy mental curiosity, thereby occupying minds by means of futile dialectics and rhetorical exposition.

Duns Scott and St. Thomas Aquinas, consequently, were the principal authors, transported from the Spanish to the Spanish American universities, although Descartes and Locke, that is, Rationalism and Sensualism, were not unknown in the New World, for these ideas seem to have been discussed in Mexico by the priest Gamarra [10], in the eighteenth century.

Nor did the development of thought in northern Europe fail to be reflected in Spain and Portugal, but in the colonies its image was less clear, because there it was only the reflection of that other reflection. In any case, as Señor Francisco Garcia Calderon tells us in an excellent paper on the intellectual currents of Latin America presented to the Philosophical Congress of Heidelburg, and included in his volume upon "The Professors of Idealism," the Natural Law School originated new ideas about the Indians which could not fail to suggest new sentiments in regard to them, and the Cartesian Scepticism, as well as the scientific discoveries of Newton, were explained and discussed in colonial publications towards the close of the eighteenth century.

The social development of this period, which was especially fruitful in political changes, found, therefore, a field already prepared for the germinating of ideas of liberty of thought and democratic liberty of the French philosophers. Their extreme theories, through their very violence, were more acceptable to spirits ready to give eager welcome to revolutionary ideas than the well-weighed opinions of Washington, Adams and Hamilton, and even of Jefferson, who not having been in vain a compatriot and contemporary of Franklin, passed these European extravagancies through the sieve of his wholesome poise and solid good sense.

It was men educated in the principles of this greatest of revolutions—principles, however, now partially modified by the Napoleonic restoration of order—whom the colonies sent to the Constitutional Cortes of Cadiz and Lisbon, to be the interpreters of their culture and aspirations, and who played a conspicuous part in both of these Assemblies which, while revolutionary in origin, were practically constructive in purpose.

The Brazilian deputies who, in 1821, took their seats in the Portuguese Constituent Assembly [11], supplied the better part of the Parliamentary element of the Empire. They were not able to be present at the debates until the end, nor to defend to the utmost by word of mouth or wisdom of procedure their national rights, because the ill-treatment of their colleagues and the insults of the populace were insufferable. The separation of the two countries was becoming more clearly defined across the seas. In proportion as the old country tried to place the new kingdom of Brazil under former colonial dependence, the breach kept widening, and the circle of complete rupture closing in. It was thus that the liberal Portuguese attempted to put liberty in practice.

In Spain, the situation was somewhat different. On the one hand the Colonies had given proof of Unionist sympathies in the worst of the crisis, both by resisting the seductions of French agents, such as that Marquis de Sassenay who was appointed by Napoleon to Buenos Aires then under the Viceroy Liniers [12], as well as by the gift of ninety millions to aid in the expenses of the Peninsular War. On the other hand, in spite of the admitted and recognized principles of perfect political and civil equality between Spaniards and Americans being denied in practice, and in spite of the merchants of Cadiz having secured the revocation of the decree of freedom of commerce between the colonial possessions and foreign countries, there was in Spain, nevertheless, a certain feeling that sympathized with at least some of the colonial aspirations, some expression of which we meet with even in official documents.

While in Portugal jealousy prevailed because Brazil had become the seat of monarchy and because the King was apparently well satisfied to remain there, in Spain, a common evil, that of the lack of a legitimate sovereign and subjection to foreign dominion, in the one case actually existing, in the other virtually so, tended to draw the mother country and colonies into closer relations. As a matter of fact, in 1810 many people, even those of the Peninsula, believed the old Spanish independence to be irrevocably lost; but the excuse given for the hostility of the American possessions to the Regency at Cadiz was that their vote and opinion had not been taken in its organization. The declaration of Caracas stated most clearly that the Spaniards across the sea were not colonists, but integral parts of the Spanish Kingdom, and as such, upon the fall of the monarch, they were called upon to exercise provisional sovereignty.

The Spanish-American representatives at the Cortes of Cadiz, because of what has been indicated, were more fortunate in the beginning than the Brazilian delegation at Lisbon. It fell to the lot of the former to act as a pendulum, oscillating between antagonistic opinions, holding the balance of power and playing a part similar to that of the Irish party in the present House of Commons, precisely dealing with the identical question of "Home Rule."

The over-sea deputies voted naturally with the Liberals in questions touching great reforms of common interest, but in matters of practical or current legislation they occasionally joined with the opposite party. A Spanish historian writes that they put a price on their support, for they always exacted as advance payment, some concession which it was often impossible to grant, giving it to be understood that thus trafficking with their votes, they hoped to accomplish through Parliament almost the same for their country, or one might say for their countries, as the insurgents at the front were fighting for. The fact is that if the reforms attempted at that time had been realized earlier, the separation would have at least suffered great delay, for such reforms involved a political bond similar to that which binds Canada and Australia to the British Crown. However, history records what was, not what ought to have been. In one of the beautiful "National Episodes" of the Spanish novelist Perez Galdos, there figures a personage whose ambition is to write a History of Spain to suit the ideals to which she should have attained.[2] Quixotism could scarcely be carried to greater lengths. In this imaginative history, Ferdinand VII, after being sentenced and ordered to be shot, is described as marching to punishment to the roll of arms and appealing to the judgment of posterity. How different was the reality—a disloyal king strangling every attempt at representative rule. For the Cortes of Cadiz was quite different from the ancient Spanish Cortes. This latter body, like the analogous institution of Portugal, never really represented the entire country, but only those cities, towns, corporations, or individuals, that through merit or favor had attained to such right. Nevertheless, while there were in the older times classes that still remained servants of those classes who were able to appear in the Cortes and claim immunities and privileges, in this manner affecting the social equilibrium, a principle new to these Peninsular gatherings, that of national sovereignty, was affirmed by the Assemblies at Cadiz and Lisbon. In fact the first act of the Spanish Cortes was to assume such sovereignty, declaring null and void the ceding of the Crown of Spain in Napoleon's favor, "not only because of the violence which had characterized the unjust and illegal acts of Bayonne, but principally because the consent of the people was wanting." The people had finally risen for the restoration of national dignity, honor, and liberties, at the same time that they were restoring the national monarchy.

If in Spain, Fernando VII acted in relation to the Parliamentary movement as he acted in every emergency, namely, with hypocrisy and malice, in Portugal Dom John VI, who was immeasurably more intelligent and good-hearted, lacked energy enough either to remedy the excesses of the demagogues or to check the absolutist reaction. His natural weakness of character here reached its most acute stage. The result was that whether because of the procedure of their sovereigns or because of deeply-rooted instincts which demanded that patriotism be uncompromising, the

---

[2] This same method of investing history with the garb of romance has been successfully applied to the United States—with even a smaller admixture of fiction—by your author Edwin Markham in his series "The Real America in Romance."

Spanish and Portugese Kingdoms showed themselves to be deaf to the voice of political justice in spite of the fact that this would have resulted in equal advantage to both of them. The separation took place in Spanish America under conditions of unusual violence, leaving a bitterness of animosity even in Portuguese America. In the state of mind subsequent to and determined by this chief event, which created in both communities a situation identical in nature, only different in intensity, we trace the origin of the intellectual aspect peculiar to Latin America during the last century. In any consideration of the prolongation of the Latin civilization to the over-seas countries, the circumstances under which the separation was effected inevitably assume a certain importance. This is especially true as regards both the distinctive form given to literary expression by the temperamental peculiarities of the colonists, as well as the local traditions already long established for so new a country.

Among the Spanish descendants, who were more warlike by nature, and whose struggle for independence had been more obstinate, it was natural that the heroic element should prevail. The stanzas of Olmedo, celebrating the victories of Junin and Ayacucho, symbolize the poetic school evolved by this patriotic sentiment which had as its ultimate expression in prose the work entitled "Venezuela Heroica," of Don Eduardo Blanco [13], a brilliant writer whom his country crowned just before his death. Bolívar is always the epic figure which evokes the memory of the not far-distant past: the Spaniard was at that period the target for all sorts of maledictions. "War to the Usurper," exclaims the Inca Huaina Capac [14], when he appears before the conquerors on the night of Junin. "Do we, perchance, owe him for any benefits—light, customs, laws, religion? No, nothing! He was ignorant, full of vices, fierce, superstitious. His faith, atrocious blasphemy, is not the faith of Christ. Blood, lead, steel, these are his saints, his dearest sacraments."

Among the descendants of Portugal who were more sentimental by nature and whose emancipation was almost bloodless, Indianism or the idealizing of the Savage as the heroic type, predominates. Indeed, this was not entirely unknown in Spanish America, where it served as inspiration to some of her best poets, such as Juan Leon Mera of Ecuador, the author of the "Virgin of the Sun"[15]. However, the tendency was not so general as in Brazil, where it is prominent in the best writers—in verse, in the lyrics of Gonçalves Dias, in prose, in the novels of José de Alencar [16]—coming to be a recognized feature of the national literature, at least in its most flourishing period, that of Romanticism. In the poet, the

Indian sentiment was more natural and spontaneous because of the admixture of Portugese and Indian in his blood; more conventional and artificial, but none the less beautifully expressed, in the prose writer who was of pure European race. But in both, the tendency was the same, and the most competent of Brazilian critics, Sr. José Verissimo [17], defines it in the following extract, from one of his volumes on "Studies in Brazilian Literature."

"For the first time our poetry breathes the pungent odors and soft perfumes of our virgin forest, the air of our campos, the affected, sensual sentimentality of our amorous passions, of our griefs . . . something in fact, that was thoroughly native—our popular poetry, our ballads, risen as it were, to the level of great poetry, imbuing it with their sentiment and melancholy. The idealizing of the savage awoke in our souls for the first time some feeling for these unfortunate creatures, and the Romance reaction, exaggerating it, bestowed upon it a chivalric and glorious aspect."

In both these Brazilian writers, the greatest of the Romantic school in their country, written expression was equally literary and polished, emphasizing the fact that both were true Purists, perfect masters of the Portuguese language. Along with this trend of zeal for pure literary form, we see the two Iberian literatures of the New World resembling each other, at least for a time. Later, in proportion as the traditions of the home-land began to loosen their hold upon the neo-Portuguese, the devotion to a common mother-country tightened its grip upon the neo-Spanish peoples.

We are treating here evidently of a bond of union purely moral, not political in its nature. Your war with Spain, which from the Spanish view-point was aggression of the stronger against the weaker, ultimately contributed towards the deepening of this characteristic, purifying a filial sentiment that is undeniably honorable. In other words, at the very time when recollections of the bloody struggle between mother-country and revolted colonies were most vivid, and strong suspicions and animosities still lingered, the love of the mother-tongue was, as it were, the outward expression of a latent devotion.

The literary men of yesterday, like those of today, stood guard over the language that had reached a beautiful maturity, and whose purity was threatened by its exotic environment; to such an extent was this true that the academies of the Spanish language founded across the seas considered themselves all as branches of the Spanish Academy, not as independent organisms; in this way establishing intimate intellectual association. The brilliant Peruvian poet, Santos Chocano [18], upon the presentation of his volume of verses "Alma America," to the King of Spain, says with emphasis in his dedication that the language of Cervantes availed more than the arm of Columbus to make him monarch of that fruitful Eden, and he adds with spirit, that the sons of Occidental India had for three hundred years looked upon the author of Don Quixote as the best of their viceroys.

In Brazil, the Purist tradition is far from being equally reverenced today: or rather it has been fading little by little among the scholars, and it is to them that I naturally allude here. The Academy of Letters at Rio de Janeiro, modeled after the French Academy, had as its aim to dedicate itself to the future Brazilian language, rather than to the ancient Portuguese tongue, and even if we do count among our number a writer such as Ruy Barbosa [19], master of all the secrets, artifices, peculiarities, modulations, and idioms of the language of our European ancestors, an equal of that great Jesuit of the XVII century, Antonio Vieira [20], both rivals in verbal invention, the fact is due more to individual caprice than to a general race sentiment.

Nevertheless, the earliest Portuguese lexicographer, Moraes Silva [21], who is still regarded as an authority and who rendered accessible the prolix, erudite work of the Abbé Bluteau [22], was a Brazilian of colonial times, and, after the Independence of Brazil, the grammarians of Maranhão enjoyed merited fame. At this same time, however, there was spreading the doctrine that a new nationality should not only have its special literature, but a distinguishing language. Literature thus lent a hand also in forging weapons against the former mother-country in the political arsenal of Time,—weapons with which to oppose whatever might have remained of its moral preponderance.

This feature of hostility was infinitely less pronounced among the nations of Spanish descent who even found in a common literary Past one of the strongest claims of their respective personalities. From the international point of view they discovered moreover in this equality the germ of a future Iberian-American Union. One might say that the intellectual harmony in this case was always exerting itself towards a counteracting of the tendency to political dispersion.

No better representative of this disposition ever lived than the aforementioned Rufino José Cuervo [23], the late distinguished Colombian philologist and a patriot whose love of country was above question. A profound student of Spanish letters, both ancient and modern, in his famous "Dictionary of Construction and Rules" he has made an admirable study of the Spanish language, with all its richness, its rules and peculiarities, accepting the inevitable American provincialisms at the same time that he defends the traditional character of the original language.

Although not written with this object, this work constitutes in itself a lively protest against the conviction previously set forth by the author that the Spanish language would be broken up and transformed in the same way as the Latin was broken up into the Romanic languages, the provincialisms thus destroying the old idiomatic unity. In this connection, it does not strike me as a happy inference which Cuervo draws in regard to the English of the United States and Great Britain, because it seems to me that I note on the part of their cultivated people—but I am unable to say whether or not my theory leads me into error—a tendency towards philological approximation. Even though this tendency is found only among an intellectual minority, that is no reason why it may not prevail, but rather the contrary, since the victory always falls to the daring minorities.

In both cases, the study of the national origins tends to draw them together. It is by allying this sentiment of a collective and remote character with the individual and local sentiment, incorporating the national instinct with the patriotic, that the Peruvian poet, Santos Chocano, rises to his beautiful effective synthesis, in which he refers to his poems as Indo-Spanish, and styles himself "Poet of America," well meriting what another great neo-Spanish poet, Ruben Dario [24], has said of him:—

> "El tiene el Amazonas y domina los Andes:
> Siempre funde su verso para las cosas grandes:
> Va, como Don Quijote, en ideal campaña;
> Vive de amor de America y de pasión de España."

Translation of Mr. Howell:—

> "His hold is on the Amazon; o'er the Andes is his sway;
> His Muse to naught but great things attunes her note, alway;
> Side by side with Don Quixote, waging an ideal campaign,
> His Love—it is America; his Passion—it is Spain."

It is with such noted devotees that Spanish American poetry proved, in spite of its traditionalism, to be superior to contemporary Spanish poetry, acquiring at the same time, marked individuality. It is only fair to state however that its models were not exclusively Peninsular. The French intellectual influence predominates in all Latin America during the nineteenth century, in politics as in literature, in poetry as in philosophy.

Lamartine, Alfred de Musset and Victor Hugo were freely imitated across the seas in what pertains to their sentimental emotion, their ardent sensualism, their verbal brilliancy. Benjamin Constant set the stamp of his constitutional theory upon the monarchy of Brazil, at the same time that the doctrinarianism of Guizot, with all its liberal austerity, was constantly being invoked in other countries where military anarchy reaped the benefit of political aspirations. The Eclecticism of Victor Cousin was, at this time, the favorite philosophical cult of those who allowed themselves to be fascinated by the charm of a refined spiritualism and the graces of an eloquent style. The impress of this amiable rhetorician was continued through his intellectual successors, Saisset, Janet and Jules Simon, until the Positivism of Auguste Comte, flourishing side by side with Spiritualism, gathered over-sea groups of enthusiastic followers, and sought to mold into distinctive and well controlled form the Latin American mentality.

There is little difficulty in tracing the English influence. We have only to go back to Don Andres Bello, a disciple of the Scotch Speculative School of Reid and Dugald Stewart, in whom Garcia Calderon points out the attributes always characteristic of an Anglo-Saxon philosopher: good sense—which a famous Portuguese satirist has called common sense—moral stoicism, and skill in analysis. In passing, we must mention the name of Stuart Mill, associated as it is with the criticism of representative rule, and we next come to the Evolutionism of Herbert Spencer. Evolutionism rivalled Positivism in popularity, that is in so far as its effect upon intellectual activity is concerned. Then the preoccupations of social problems entered to hold in check the excessive individualism, which in lyric form tinged with romantic color all political and literary expression of the first half of the nineteenth century.

Weak and uncertain in the beginning, the new mental currents exhibited humanitarian instincts corresponding to the social demands, as well as a frantic enthusiasm for progress, which is simply another phase of Idealism; subsequently, opposing all traditions, it assumed an openly anti-religious character closely associated with a devotion to science. All over Latin America the struggle between Religion and Science showed itself so uncompromising that no one would have believed possible the conciliation that soon followed, so much the less anticipated because of the old antagonisms between thought and dogma, which existed in all of these countries.

If today the government of a Garcia Moreno [25], supporting an inquisitorial dogmatism in Ecuador, is no longer possible, still less does anyone presume as did Juarez with Mexico, to attempt to change by force a clerical nation into free-thinkers or to plant lay-despotism where ecclesiastical despotism held sway. Rigidity of formula is not to be wondered at, when the theory of such transformation was wrought out in Mexico by Positivism, whose influence is felt in the mental evolution in all Latin America, especially in that of Brazil and Chile.

In Chile, in spite of the minor success of the religious orthodoxy of the apostle Lagarrigue [26], Positivism completely undermined an extremely conservative society; in Brazil, it may be charged with even more important and fundamental responsibilities for the change of Government. The Republic of Brazil was not, however, as was announced at the time with some appearance of truth, exclusively due to the influence of the doctrines of Auguste Comte [27].

As a matter of fact, this philosophical school developing into a religious system, intervened at the psychological moment to draw away a great number of army officers who were its disciples into association with such disaffected elements as the veterans of the Paraguayan War, offended at official neglect and at the lack of sympathy shown towards their class aspirations; the slave owners, denied any lawful indemnity for the loss of their slaves; besides those ardent propagandists dominated by their ideal, and anxious to see all America united under the same democratic rule.

Doubt, and later, materialistic negation, had prepared the way for the relative supremacy of Positivism shared as it was with that other philosophical system, whose basic expression, Evolution, had a magic sound to the ear, and whose prestige was furthered by the diffusion of Sociology, the Science of modern times in its correlation with the Natural Sciences. The idealistic reaction was, however, bound to come especially when through the deceptive paradoxes of Nietzsche positive ideas practically eventuated in an un-moral Nihilism, which was even more destructive than the bitter Pessimism of Schopenhauer.

Both of these philosophers had many disciples in Latin America. This was due partly to the apparent novelty of their deceptive theories ultimately based, though they were, upon ancient Greek philosophy,— theories which were dangerously seductive and proved to be irresistible to many because of the freedom of their teachings, especially as contrasted with the dogmatic limitations of Positivism. The fascination lent by success to the German influence from both an economic and intellectual standpoint also accounts in part for the temporary popularity of these two representatives of modern German thought.

In Brazil, it was Tobias Barreto [28], the greatest representative of Germanism in the realm of thought, who about 1880 reformed the teaching of Law, stripping it of the artificiality of its supposed inherent metaphysics, in order to give it the character of a civilizing agency. In spite of its scientific methods of expression, the effect of this intellectual current was to promote the revival of Idealism, which is a preponderant feature of the German temperament, and which we may even say, lies at the base of all European mentality, of which the American is simply a continuation. What has presided over the moral evolution of the New World, if not Idealism? Its intellectual emancipation was determined by ideas of justice, of liberty, of human rights, and of progress, which France sent to it, clothed in a philosophical drapery, to which England gave substantial form in her model development, and which in the Iberian Peninsula, awoke old and slumbering echoes. The religious austerity of the English Pilgrims, the visionary daring of the Spanish conquerors, the highly wrought imagination tinged with melancholy of the Brazilian pioneers,— what were these but so many aspects of Idealism, an hereditary instinct that material demands could not eliminate, but which the hardships of colonial life and the general tendency of subsequent periods had tended to disguise?

The spell of science as the only guide of the spirit having once been broken, it was not strange that in Latin America Fouillée, with his social determinism, Guyau, with his scientific Spiritualism, Bergson, with his new metaphysics, should have become the intellectual idols displacing the old fetishes,—Taine, Renan, Haeckel, the exponents of concrete analysis, of philosophical doubt, and naturalistic synthesis.

The psychological method has been steadily driving out Positivism, the solutions of which do not seem deep enough to satisfy our mental aspirations. The human spirit soars higher, and whether it be because of its peculiar nature, or whether on account of its long upward evolution, it demands more complex analyses, seeks to penetrate more deeply into the secret of things, demands syntheses of a higher nature. Science of itself is not sufficient to satisfy such demands. How then could Poetry be included within its range?

In Brazil we had scientific poetry based upon investigation and inspired by progress, but Love once more holds her place under the source of lyric inspiration. Romance, in its turn, was no longer under the control of those purely physiological influences with which the Naturalism of Flaubert, Zola and Maupassant, had imbued it, but now based its action more on suggestions which, whether religious or social, in any case, were psychological. The Venezuelan, Diaz Rodríguez [29], and the Brazilian, Coelho Netto [30], for example, who are considered masters of the contemporaneous Latin American novel, may be Realists in their methods, but they certainly are Idealists in their tendencies.

Idealism in Latin America, however, as Garcia Calderon says, has to contend with certain difficulties, commencing with the absence of such Individualism as is found in the Anglo-Saxon (I always mean in such case Anglo-American) who expresses his inner life in a form of conscious thought and action that makes Religion an inner sentiment, rather than an outward show. Moreover, education in Latin America is on a lower level than here among you. Political life is far from possessing the same stability. Economic questions, on the other hand, attain to greater importance; at least there is more of the human in their signification, since there is much less wealth than in the United States, and a much greater distance between rich and poor. Here your rich are richer, but your poor are generally less poor.

Nevertheless, in spite of all this, Idealism still advances amongst us, and at the same time religious sentiment is growing deeper, raising the standard of education, purifying politics, and tending to correct inequalities of fortune. With the aid of intellectual curiosity, which is great, and a no less vigorous power of assimilation, there is no reason why Idealism should be impeded in its program toward settled beliefs, or fail to reach the regions of pure speculation, eliminating the social feature which has so conspicuously permeated constructive philosophy.

The essential nature of Idealism is naturally a desire to soar high, and this desire has taken possession of the Latin American spirit. If its aspirations are so high as to cause a smile, seeing that they are so out of proportion to the means at its command, and altogether out of accord with present conditions, still this very ambition is the best guarantee for its future. A race without ideals is a dying race, destined to servitude, if not to final extinction. This can never be the case with Latin America. She has already acquired a personality of her own, whose literary expression at least in the realm of poetry, is already superior of that of the former mother countries.

The poetry of our lands began by imitating the French, but it has since come to be distinctively American. The following remarks by Blanco Fombona [31] apply as truly to Spanish as to Portuguese America:

"We have given new wings to the old lyric songster, and having broken loose from Peninsular traditions, we no longer dash off album madrigals, hymns to the child Jesus, couplets for blind beggars, hand-kissing ballads, and warlike odes, but sing with as much beauty and individuality as we can the truth of our brain, our heart, our eyes, what we have thought, have felt, have seen. . . . Modernism, as a school, commenced by being an echo of what was foreign, but soon, thanks to our individualistic character, it changed to an accentuation of personalities outside of any common creed, and to a search for and exaltation of truly American themes, at times subjective, expressing the emotion of American hearts, at times objective, studying our nature, our history, the customs of our countries."

I have already called your attention to the fact that side by side with this formation of a political personality with the aid of literature, there was a growing devotion to a Past common to the mother country and the colonies in Spanish America, a worship of the glories of their race.

This characteristic was as honorable as it was peculiar to them, for I have never found even among you or among us Brazilians any national poet celebrating England or Portugal as Santos Chocano exalts Spain in the following lines:

> "Tú si eres grande,
> España remanesca y luminosa;
> tú eres la Fé que al corazon expande;
> tú, la Esperanza que en la Fé reposa;
> y tú, la Caridad que por doquiera
> va prodigando su alma generosa.
> Grande fué tu ideal, grande tu ensueño;
> tan grande fuiste en la Christiana Era.
> Que el mundo antiguo resultó pequeño
> y para tí se completó la Esfera."

Translation by Mr. Howell:—

> "O Spain! breathing Romance; Spain, gleaming with light;
> Faith art thou ever, to clothe hearts with Might;
> Hope art thou ever, in Faith's spring finding course;
> Charity, with lavish gifts strewing thy course;
> Great were thine ideals, in pointing the way;
> So great in the age of Christianity's sway.
> So great that the Old World too small doth appear,
> And a New World is needed to round out thy Sphere."

LECTURE VI.

Moral integration produced by the fusion of the races, the condition of social equilibrium.—The historic episode of Bolívar and Pétion.—Disadvantages of intermarriage, which gives rise to a great difference in ideals.—Political unrest of Latin America, formerly the hope of the European democracy.—Causes of the revolutionary disturbances.—The anarchical and conservative elements in the Iberian societies of the New World.—Bolívar's conception and its realization in Brazil.—Strength of traditionalism.—Historic function of the Brazilian Monarchy.—Federation and the rule of dictators.—Private initiative and the work of education and moralization.—Liberty and tyranny.—Troubles in the evolutionary march of the Peoples across the sea.—Lack of harmony between the theory and practice, between the régime and the people.—The Brazilian oligarchy during the empire and its mission.—Political regeneration through social education and economic development.—Mariano Moreno and Dom John VI.—Industrialism and the emancipation of the people.—Violence and culture.—Qualities, services and glories of Latin America.—The American conscience and Pan-Americanism.—America for humanity.

THE fusion of the races inhabiting Latin America is a forceful factor in that moral integration which represents the fusion of sentiments —an integration deeper and consequently more significant than either political association or literary union, since the former might be actuated by self-interest and the latter be merely the result of a worship of form or love of the beautiful. Race fusion produces a state of social equilibrium which will become stable as soon as differences in education are corrected and reality takes the place today occupied by imagination expressing itself in verbosity. And this same fusion constitutes the basis for a cordial union which, as we have already had occasion to verify, represents a tradition and is one of the best guarantees of the future of these lands of Spanish-Portuguese civilization.

During the colonial period in Brazil, the dominion of the Dutch, which with Pernambuco as its capital comprised an empire extending from the Amazon to the São Francisco, was overthrown and the Portuguese power reëstablished by the joint efforts of the whites, Indians and negroes, who fought in separate regiments, but under the same flag, the same command and with the same object. The regiments of the three races which formed the national population, worked together for the reconquest of the territory, and their chiefs, regardless of their color, were equally recompensed, honored and ennobled by the government of the mother country [1].

One of the ceremonies attending the celebration of the One Hundredth Anniversary of the Independence of Venezuela was the inauguration of a monument to Alexandre Pétion [2], the negro President of Haiti who did not hesitate to welcome the exiled Bolívar and supply him with vessels, arms, ammunition, provisions, money, and even with a printing-press for the sacred enterprise of emancipating the continent from slavery such as that in which this zealous lover of human liberty had been. The only condition which the precursor of Lincoln imposed upon the emulator of Washington in exchange for his valuable services, was that all those in the Spanish colonies who were not yet citizens with rights equal to the freedmen should be set free. Bolívar and Pétion thus offered the foundation of a truly liberal America in which might be effected by peaceful means that union of the nations towards which Bolívar ever strove. This same dream of a great union of free peoples has been aptly described by the well known Venezuelan writer Carlos Zumeta, the author of *Continente enfermo* [3] as the Babel vision, for he sees in it the reënactment of the biblical myth of the nations of the earth coming together and speaking a single tongue even as it was before the fatal confusion provoked by pride.

The conception of what constitutes a race has undergone various modifications and interpretations. There are many people who object to the distinction between superior and inferior races, and such an objection may be well taken when the expression is applied to different types of the same race, as Latins and Germans. On the other hand, such a distinction cannot be denied in view of historical evolution itself, in treating, for example, of Europeans and Africans. The intermarriage of the races was morally and socially a backward step for Latin America, whose greatest defect has been precisely the lack of harmony, one might almost say, the incompatability between the splendid ideals which individually and collectively have been formed for it, and the petty aspirations of certain component parts of the new race or sub-race which was formed by fusion in its territory. Those ideals were not spontaneous or natural to the people who had adopted and embraced them; they were borrowed and conventional, and hence their ineffectiveness in this case as a means of elevation. A Bolivian writer, who has applied the epithet *sick* to the people of his country, and had thus thought to contribute to the psychology of the Spanish American peoples, has said on this point that "the seductive principles which produced the rights of man were the prime cause of the restless institutional life of our people, because they were *taken* as ideals, but not felt; and an ideal whose roots do not go down deep into the consciousness, does not tend to be easily realized, because it does not constitute a necessity of the spirit." [1]

Indeed, these peoples needed other more simple therapeutics to cure them of the malady which has given rise to the greatest accusation made against Latin America, that of their political and social unrest. The opinion of Europe and that of your country also is at one with the belief that they are suffering from an incurable revolutionary fever, whose periodicity is but another symptom of its pathological nature. Neither the orderly example of the Empire of Brazil, whose traditions the Republic endeavored to preserve although it did not succeed in avoiding collisions, which were natural and inevitable in the work of adapting the nation to the new régime of a revolutionary origin, nor the peaceful and highly progressive evolution of some of the Spanish-American Republics during the last decades, have succeeded in dissipating that impression which time alone will be able to correct and even entirely undo, for time undoes everything, especially when of itself the effect ceases.

The ancient European monarchies could only congratulate one another on the result of the experiment, and the exultation felt by those of anti-democratic sentiment, over this sorry example was in proportion to the hopes that had been reposed in the future of the essentially Republican continent, where now alone flourished, transplanted from a different flora, the so-called "exotic plant" of the Brazilian monarchy. Latin America had its hour of general popularity when the Abbé de Pradt [4] discovered there the reserve of the worn-out society of Europe. Your virtues of the first period—the heroic age of democracy—associated as they were to be with our wealth, real or latent, but which European imagination exaggerated, seemed to promise a most prosperous and brilliant future for the New World, which was supposed to become a refuge for the persecuted thought and desperate poverty of the Old World.

In discussing a political feature which has already disappeared in a part of Spanish America, we may look at the subject from an historical, as well as social standpoint. I shall therefore begin by having recourse to the South American treatise on sociology, *Le Pérou contemporain,* by Francisco Garcia Calderon, and apply the author's reflections on the evolution of his country in the nineteenth century, to the remainder of the former Spanish colonial empire after it had achieved its independence.

"Throughout the entire century militarism favors anarchy, and the activities of the nation are concentrated in politics, in struggles for power.

---

[1] A. Argüedas, *Pueblo Enfermo.*

The Constitution, engrafted on the French text, does not reach the soul of the people. Ancient formulas, secular instincts continue, and the power becomes despotic and labor continues to be an inferior occupation. Bachelors of law and of science exercise the power jointly with the chiefs of the army: there is a dynasty of scholars as in the Orient. Wealth increases, thanks to guano and nitrate; life seems easy and free from care; the State plays the part of administrator of fortunes; prodigality increases; the gold mirage disturbs the mental equilibrium. Bankruptcy and the War of the Pacific [6] consummate the previous work of dissolution. The history of half a century is nothing but an unbridled seeking for wealth, amid the instability of things and the ambitious conflicts of men. It is only in the last decade that life changes its aspect, peace becomes final and one notes a more or less clearly defined progress in political and social forms."

Except for the splendor and wealth of Peru and the dramatic incidents connected with its foreign war—periods of great magnificence and great humiliation which were peculiar to this country—the history of the Spanish-American Republics in the past century is singularly alike, apart, of course from the local coloring which distinguishes, for example, an Argentine *gaucho* [7] from a Peruvian aristocrat, or a Chilian *roto* [8] from a Venezuelan *llanero* [9]. The difference of class, the nature of the soil, the diversity of industries, pastoral, mining, agricultural, etc., here as elsewhere served to modify outward appearances, but at bottom the people had the same psychology and an identical conception of the commonwealth *(res publica)*.

At first the political mould adjusted itself badly to the condition of the nations for whose use it had been cut, in accordance with the fashion plate. The prejudice of a Constitution based on European principles, an organic law laying down fixed rules and *a priori* solutions for the conduct of affairs, did not fit in well with the inferior, vacillating and transitory character of the societies which it had to govern and for which it had been conventionally framed. The inferior character of the population, the rabble which did not deserve the name of people, offered truly a splendid field for the cultivation of obedience, but of a passive and so-to-speak unconscious obedience. The very soil was suited to the acclimatization of despotic militarism, on account of the absence of the sentiment of individuality, the predominance of the collective instincts and race traditions.

Sr. Garcia Calderon aptly describes the situation in these concise words: "A profound legality terminated the revolutionary conquest. The dead, however, continued to exert a powerful influence. For a long time the Republic was still but a kind of State socialism. It imposed its will on individual energies for the execution of the reforms undertaken through its strong initiative. The richness of the soil made life easy on account of its abundant yield. The periodical revolutions did not make any changes save in the outward appearance of things. The obscure soul of the people remained unconscious because of its absolute lack of culture and want of vigor."

At a given moment there came a change of scene, for reasons different from those prevailing had provoked a subversive movement. The campaign which, from interested motives, professional agitators were making, was having its effect; their hollow but pernicious phrases were performing their work; the people were being incited to greed; the pseudo-conscience of the political destinies of the country was awakening. Thus for a brief time agitation triumphed over passivity, rebellion over automatism, anarchy over homogeneity. By continuing this contest of tendencies between individuals, some of them half-breeds, and one or the other tendency predominating according as the character of the person expressing it was more nearly like the one or the other original factor, all being subjected to the same influence of culture, Spanish individualism was reborn in the same "excess of movement" which, in the felicitous words of a Castilian writer, transferring action to the literary field, produced the theater of Calderon, Lope de Vega and Tirso de Molina.

Bolívar, with the farsightedness of his genius, foresaw the political disorder resulting from a social confusion which found active expression in an army governed by ambitious military leaders who wished to transform it into a Praetorian guard, and passive expression in a population in reality divided into castes, although theoretically equal by the declaration of a common sovereignty. Hence it was his idea to give the greatest prestige to the conservative element, which had become neutral by force of circumstances and showed a tendency to disappear in the abyss of the successive disturbances of the public order. These ideas of his are invariably reflected throughout all the constructive phases of his public life, from the suggestion, made to the constituent Congresses of Colombia, of 1819 and 1821, of the creation of an hereditary Senate and moral power, to the incorporation in the project of the Bolivian Constitution of 1826 of an irresponsible president elected for life, and of a third chamber composed of censors likewise holding their positions for life. The functions of such an assembly would be to protect the national culture, guard morality and the Constitution, collaborate in the public treaties, and choose the judges and ecclesiastical dignitaries from triple lists submitted by the Senate. Thus in it would reside the moderating power.

The Brazilian Empire, with its constitutional sovereign, its dynasty acclaimed by the people, its Senate elected for life and composed of the finest men of the country, the spirit of its administration, at once conservative and liberal, largely and wisely realized the ideas of Bolívar, which were chimerical in view of their falsely democratic environment as well as the personal reluctance of the great man to wear the trappings as well as the attributes of the dictator. Moreover, the maintenance on the throne of the traditional dynasty representing the Portuguese past, whose heir, however, identified himself with the new destinies of the country and even made himself the decisive agent of its independence, not only removed the crown of Brazil from the conflict of ambitions, but gave the national traditions a strength and importance unique, compared with what occurred in the neighboring countries of the new Spanish world. The revolutions of which Brazil was the theater during the first reign and the Regency represented, therefore, ideas, although expressed by passions, rather than the greed of power. For many reasons, the Brazilian monarchy in the nineteenth century may be said to have been the political régime truly suited to the social status of Latin America.

Traditionalism, which if not a stronger sentiment, at least is more in evidence among us than it is among you; which strikes its roots, if not in a richer, at least in a more dramatic legendary and heroic past than yours, and which is reflected especially in picturesque and charming cities, breathing an incomparable perfume of things gone by, such as Lima in Peru and Ouro Preto [10] in Brazil, the only ones of their kind in America, is naturally strengthened under such a régime and becomes capable of developing a great power of resistance to the destroying instincts of the lower strata of society. This was the case with the Empire of Brazil which yielded to the revolutionary shock and dissolved itself politically, preserving, however, its structure, whch in this case was its moral wholeness.

The monarchy of Brazil fully realized its function as protector of the rights and privileges of the uncultivated and therefore powerless masses, who intrusted themselves to it in order not to be despoiled and tortured by intriguing and pitiless oligarchies which were shortsighted and actuated by the most selfish motives. Thus it was that it succeeded in representing, in Latin America, domestic peace and liberty at a time when a condition of anarchy prevailed in nearly all the rest of the continent. That which the Caesarism of Bolívar failed to attain, owing to his repugnance to what a Venezuelan author calls the liberty-destroying temptation, a repugnance which we have seen was largely the fruit of his own worship of his glory as a Liberator, the Empire of Dom Pedro accomplished completely. The unity of Brazil came out triumphant from the test, in striking contrast to the fiasco of the attempted organization of a great Spanish American nation or confederation, a fiasco all the more felt since as Señor Blanco Fombona [11], the Venezuelan author, well says, the small countries are the heel of Achilles of Spanish America.

But from the splendid dream of Bolívar, which only could have been realized under a monarchy, as the example of Portuguese America proves, there was born that noble inspiration of the Congress of Panama, already mentioned, in which arbitration was outlined as the supreme principle of American Public Law. This moral result amply redeems its political failure.

In South America, after it had become independent and had been freed also from its Napoleons in perspective—for as you know one of them, San Martin, had retired, worn out, to Boulogne in France, and the other, exhausted and profoundly disillusioned, died at an early age at Santa Marta in Colombia—there began to have great vogue a political expression borrowed from your constitutional organization—the principle of Federalism. Only in unified Brazil, however, did this principle correspond to the legitimate aspiration of those honestly opposed to the contrary doctrine of centralization, unless, of course, one associates this sentiment of particularism with the reaction against Bolívar's plans of dominion, a reaction by means of which Paez [12] separated Venezuela from Great Colombia, and Santander [13] had recourse to abuses of power in the very year of the Liberator's death.

This same principle of federalism, in whose name Rosas [14] tyrannized over Argentina, and in opposition to which Portales [15] modeled Chile, runs like a red thread through the political history of Latin America. Federalism and centralization, however, did nothing more than justify the same disorders and the same violent acts. What remained at bottom was individualism under the picturesque garb of the military dictatorship which served to conceal it [16]. And this dictatorship (*caudillismo*) we see now imbued with a primitive rural democracy, crude and cruel, such as was that of Rosas in Argentina; now with pretensions to splendor and colonial chivalry, as was that of Castilla [17] in Peru; now solitary and ascetic, as was that of Francia [18] in Paraguay; now wildly extravagant and grotesque as was that of Santa Anna [19] in Mexico; now polished and fond of protocol, as was that of Guzman Blanco [20] in Venezuela; now brutal and intoxicated, as was that of Melgarejo [21] in Bolivia; now tinged with religious mysticism, as was that of Garcia Moreno [22] in Ecuador; now progressive and businesslike, as was that of Porfirio Diaz in Mexico. Blanco Fombona thus admirably sums up the situation: "The *cacique* rules, and over him frequently the pettifogger, the charlatan, whom the bearded chief admires and the illiterate people applaud."

To talk of federalism where the individual element is everything seems one of the most absurd things in the world, for individualism in such cases unites much better with centralization, a moderate or tyrannical expression of order, while federalism, once stripped of its ideal or traditional meaning, is nothing more than the flag of disorder. In imperial Brazil, the alternative of the historical cadence required that the federalist aspiration should correspond to particularism, which had been the basis of the administrative organization of the colony. In the Spanish-American republics, decentralization seemed to some the condition, to others the corrective for that which, although mitigated by the Revolution, was the political régime of these countries until time and such factors as the development of the public wealth, the diffusion of culture and the formation of an eminent minority of strong thinkers began to exercise their influence.[2]

When George Clemenceau, the distinguished French statesman, made his brief visit to the east coast of South America, he was not long in discovering the faults and virtues of the political societies with which he came in contact, and in which he discovered, moreover, the environment where the Latin spirit will in future shine with an ardent flame. In referring to the incapacity of the electoral body of these countries to organize the defense of the general interest against the coalitions of private interests, the writer says that he rejoiced for Argentina that abuses such as those which in greater or lesser degree are found in the old countries, and whose surest remedy consists in the development of private energies, should have been able to have aroused in that young society such manifestations of conscience and will as those he found there. And the veteran parliamentarian, whose principal fault is certainly not want of energy, adds the following commentary, full of consolation and hope: "A country, whatever may be its form of government, is strong only through its men, that is, through the sum total of its disinterested energies. Now a people capable of producing men of the intelligence and character of those I frequently met with during my trip, can confidently face the problems of the future" [23].

---

[2] These factors are admirably brought out by Blanco Fombona in his lectures given at Madrid, already cited.

The War of Independence had left the ancient Spanish American Empire in a pitiful state of devastation. It was necessary for it to reconstruct its sources of wealth, and to create new ones in order to meet its responsibilities. The protracted struggle had left it also owing to the lack of popular instruction with the worst of anarchies, an anarchy without culture, as the foundation of the national representation, which was sovereignty only in name. As a part of the same blighting heritage were those habits of public dishonesty which, frequent under the mother country's rule, were propagated among the new rulers in spite of the denunciations and objurgations of the publicists who from force of circumstances embodied the *moral power* which Bolívar dreamed of making the axis of his constitutional organization.

All the half-realized work of educating and moralizing the people, which is and must be the formula necessary to maintain Latin America's autonomy, was perhaps greater than that of the conquest or of that of the independence, because it had to contend with a stronger feature of the local past.

This new Latin American world was called suddenly without the elements necessary for readjustments to the responsibilities and dignity of international life. Need we wonder then that the newly acquired political liberty ushered in a period of social chaos. And yet from this same chaotic mass there was loosed a constellation of nations guided by principles not only of liberty, which ill-understood and worse applied had produced that chaos, but also of authority, without which societies wreck entirely and end with dissolution. Now just as liberty easily runs the risk of degenerating into anarchy, authority without moral curbs which guarantee legal curbs, borders generally on despotism: hence the wild oscillation of the magnetic needle between the quadrants as if it could not find its direction under the action of native and foreign influences. And if the native influences spoke of subjection and of revolt, the foreign ones in the nineteenth century were more than ever disposed to revolt and reaction.

Thus we see public instruction made gratuituous and compulsory in societies where the leaders of the movement were entirely lacking in culture and where the necessary number of teachers were sought in vain; we see the Church deprived by law of its privileges in countries such as Mexico, where it owned, according to Humboldt, four-fifths, and, according to the historian Lucas Alaman [24], one half of the property of the country, valued at 300 millions of dollars; and we see the death penalty for political crimes abolished, and the guarantee of individual rights "raised to the highest limits to which philosophy has aspired," in countries where each year generals were shot for the crime of sedition and citizens were imprisoned for the crime of expressing their opinions. The great defect of the Spanish American Republics—and Brazil has gravitated toward this planetary system—was the lack of harmony between theory and practice, and the resulting want of balance between the abstract and concrete. The intermarriage of the races, which characterized the Iberian colonization across the sea, is chiefly responsible for this result. The Anglo-Saxon population which was transplanted to North America and there propagated itself, was and continues to be fundamentally the same people as that of the mother country, and consequently their institutions are the same and fit to them. When fusion occurred, it was with elements of the same race; not so in the rest of the continent, where mating was effected with inferior elements, for we have seen that if there are no inferior races, there are at least inferior peoples.

These peoples were indeed without cultivation and preparation, incapable collectively of adapting themselves quickly to different and higher conditions of culture, although not so individually, for I have already had occasion to call your attention to Juarez. This pure-blooded Indian appears to us as a born legislator, a theoretical statesman, a political constructor of imagination, saturated with liberal ideas. He possessed moreover the faculty of vision in a high degree and, in the opinion of one of your writers, was lacking only in executive ability.

On the whole, the Indians of Mexico, as well as those of Bolivia, the half-breeds of Venezuela like those of Brazil, were as far from representative governments once they had gained possession of it, as were our Tupis [25], whose women prepared the buccan meat [26] for the festivities of cannibalism, or as the Aztecs, whose priests, Bernal Diaz [27] tells us, oiled their hair with the blood of human sacrifices. One can calculate the mad *farandole* which such a multitude would dance when invested in the twinkling of an eye with the attributes of sovereignty, like the people who met in the public square of Athens to discuss the affairs of the Republic, or which gathers in the Helvetian cantons to decide by *referendum* some important matter for the community.

Infinitely more *representative* of such a social state was the colonial government, whose defect consisted in being at different points refractory to progress, rather I should say in offering difficulties to the march of evolution—a forward movement which may not with impunity be opposed. The political oligarchy of the Brazilian Empire, without having this defect, was highly *representative*. It was represented by a Senate whose members were limited in number and held the position for life, and were chosen by the sovereign from triple lists made up of the names of those receiving the most votes. It was this assembly which, under the influence of the monarch—an influence exercised in fostering progress rather than moderating it—directed the destinies of the country during a period which was a model one for Latin America in the nineteenth century, a period of domestic peace, economic posterity and liberal ideas.

This oligarchy appears so little the enemy of progress that in sixty-three years—the Imperial Constitution went into effect in 1826—it left fully resolved, without the least disturbance of the public order, the fearful problem of the emancipation of the slaves which involved so many interests and resentments; it left on the way to solution the federative problem by an extended decentralization of the administration, established since 1834, as a necessary concession to the particularist tendencies; it left in application an ample foreign immigration system which will renew the population of the country, and whose effect is already so apparent that one of our most remarkable national writers already sees in Brazil a marked contrast between the country traditionally Portuguese and the cosmopolitan country where a new ethical and social type is being formed;[1] it left implanted in the soul of the people the principles of political and religious tolerance and of international generosity which have not failed to continue in the new Brazil.

Latin American progress is more pronounced in countries where, as in Brazil, a régime of order and of liberty was early established, or where, as in Argentina and Chile, the proportion of intermarriages was notably less, especially with the negro element, which was lower in the social scale, more subservient in slavery and consequently more debasing as a factor. On the other hand, the Araucanians [28], a fighting and almost indomitable race of Chile, entered largely into the composition of the warlike and stout-hearted temperament of the Chilian people.

Progress is always greater and more rapid where the white factor predominates, even in an atmosphere of disorder. The same is true where the system of government is more liberal, and, besides, more suited to the conditions of the environment, filling up with a restricted but intensive culture, the void caused by the lack of a general or extensive culture.

In the Argentine Republic the era of the periodical and fatal revolutions lasted until the war with Paraguay [29]. This condition was due to the want of education of the native element, which was commonly crude and nomadic in character, and in open conflict with the group of doctrinaires. That era, however, marked the beginning of the wonderful eco-

---

[1] José Verissimo, *Impressões do Sul*.

nomic and intellectual development of a land destined to have an extraordinary future.

How otherwise would it have been possible to bring the *gauchos*, contemporaneous with Independence, skillful cavaliers and cow-boys, given up to a life of mere vegetation on the Pampas deserts where the first great herds of cattle were bred, to a reasoned understanding of the principles of representative government which Mariano Moreno [30], certainly the most advanced and perhaps the most lucid mind of the first generation of public men of Argentina, summarized in his *Representación de los hacendados*, which in substance corresponds to the speeches of your Patrick Henry and the pamphlets of your Thomas Paine?

How is it possible to harmonize that unformed pastoral and native civilization, so different from the refined rural and cosmopolitan civilization of today, with this statement of democratic doctrine, which was based on the subordination of the government and of the laws to the interest and the will of the people and on the intervention of the latter in political affairs?

Mariano Moreno had suggested the answer to this great problem of the *Hacendados*—the producing and property owning classes—when they protested against the attitude of the *Cabildo* and Consulate of Buenos Aires in their refusal to sanction the opening of the River Plate to British commerce. It seems that the *Cabildo* and Consulate had been short-sighted enough to oppose the decision of the Viceroy Cisneros who had been sent by the Central Junta of Seville to settle local disputes and had thrown open the commerce of the River Plate to the English. This measure was not only contrary to the old Spanish ideas of exclusion, but it was all the more reasonable at this time since the English, as allies of Spain in the war against Napoleon, were already holding undisputed sway over the sea.

This same enlightened policy of commercial freedom appeared also in Portuguese America. Animated by this double motive of friendship and policy, the Portuguese Court, which had been established at Rio de Janeiro since 1808, had declared, soon after it had passed Bahia, the first Brazilian land sighted, the opening of the ports of the colony to the commerce of the world. Dom John VI and Mariano Moreno both saw the need for economic expansion of lands which were going to enter upon a new and different political life, and estimated the possibilities of such expansion. They scented modern industrialism, a term which sums up all our material, utilitarian and progressive civilization. Such a régime unquestionably offers decided advantages. It may arouse attacks because of its greedy character, which it assumes so easily, because of the voracity with which large fortunes are accumulated for the benefit of the few, while the majority remain in poverty; but to it is due, although indirectly and without speaking of the general improvement in the conditions of life, the inestimable benefit of the emancipation of the laboring class. By emancipation in this case I mean consciousness of its rights and responsibilities.

In Chile, so long as the people were represented by the despised *roto*, who slaved and spilt his blood for those above him, without receiving in exchange either consideration or elevation, and could only attenuate the hardships of his lot by becoming intoxicated and quarreling with and stabbing his comrades, there prevailed the ultra-conservative régime which gave to this society the aspect of a jealous patrician oligarchy.

Yet this oligarchical régime was not without decided advantages in the historic evolution of Chile. It was this same régime which early checked the country on its downward course of military manifestoes and civil disorganization on which it had entered, like all the rest of Spanish America soon after its independence had been assured. While its neighbor, Peru, with its great wealth, was exhausting itself in civil wars, Chile, thanks to the rigorous work synthesized in the Constitution of 1833 [31], was preparing for itself an extended period of order and material development. To its oligarchy and to the austerity which a less prosperous period implied—a period of hard work in the mines and in the fields which preceded the easily-won and abundant profits of the nitrate deposits —is really due the conquering power contained in the crystallization of Chile.

A society, however, which detains itself indefinitely at a stage of evolution which others of the same stock have already passed, is a society destined to be fatally eclipsed. An uninterrupted peace in which no ripple alters the smooth, mirror-like surface, is not of itself an exclusive guarantee of progress. Labor strikes may be a symptom of social unrest, but they are also an indication of the power of labor. Their absence indicates either a servile régime or economic atrophy.

Brazil before the abolition of slavery, the Brazil of twenty-five years ago, governed by the landed wealth which delegated its rights and powers to the class of advocates possessing a ready tongue and irresistible arguments, was certainly a more legitimate political expression of the social conditions than Brazil governed in the name of popular sovereignty by the votes of an electorate reduced by absenteeism and of which not all are equally worthy of the franchise. Was it possible meanwhile to continue slavery, the basis of that territorial wealth which was politically confined in a restricted electoral census? Is it not more worth while to pass to the faults of an epoch of more pronounced or characteristic transition? Would, moreover, the present notable economic expansion of Brazil have been compatible with colonial methods and institutions?

Certainly I do not include the throne among these institutions, for personally I consider it is possible to have a monarchy with liberty, just as it is possible to have a Republic with despotism, and I would be lacking in tolerance and intelligence if I thought otherwise. History furnishes abundant examples of both assertions and it is unnecessary for me to cite them here. I have already said more than once that Brazil under the Imperial régime enjoyed all political rights and privileges to such a degree that from this point of view, after the establishment of the Republic, there remained nothing for it to gain, but only to imitate.

Among the factors which contributed to the material development of Brazil may be mentioned a broadening of the economic foundation, a freer play of productive forces, a more varied exploitation of resources, a greater protection afforded productions—a protection which even included such advanced economic methods as those applied to coffee [32]—and finally a closer connection established between individual expression and associative methods. The political system has nothing to do with such conditions of progress, which meanwhile has gone on extending itself, for the new world is still in the growing stage. This progress may be rapid or slow, but these degrees do not affect the substance, which is regulated largely by the direction which is given to each country by the circumstances of its development. Thus, while in Brazil, thanks to the influence of tradition which at a court is tenderly cherished, however involuntary the endearments may be, literary and artistic culture was maintained more personal and more carefully cultivated. And while the same was the case in countries of Spanish America having a more dramatic past or a more intense spirituality, in Argentina letters assumed preferably a realistic tone and a scientific point of view, as one of your recent tourists to that country has observed and given expression to in picturesque *slang* [33].

This utilitarian civilization prevailing in Argentina, of which the literary qualities just mentioned are characteristic offsprings, must be the first shield of Latin America against ambitions from the outside. But no less efficacious is it against the attacks of internal enemies. Industrialism —meaning by this term not the perfect manufactured product, whose finish cannot compete with that of the European product, but the ample régime of capital in full play and under good labor conditions—will be moreover the best corrective for the armed civil strifes, of such disastrous effect, in which the restless Creole temperament has delighted and with which the early traditions of violence of these lands of adventurers has been fed.

In Brazil during colonial times, also, adventures were not wanting and the tendencies were equally violent, as our sixteenth, seventeenth and eighteenth centuries, and, later, the agitated times of the first reign and of the regency prove, but an efficient political organization through the use of authority, and particularly a prestige superior to the ambitions of the guerilla leaders, ended by establishing peace and creating a milder tradition which is endeavoring to continue. This influence, although not perfect, was highly beneficial: it made us take the lead in the open road of progress, in which other Latin-American countries, particularly the Argentine Republic, have caught up with us in recent times, thanks to the wonderful realization of her economic possibilities.

Violence therefore is yielding daily the first place to culture, or rather culture, which at no time was unknown among the Iberian societies of the New World, is gradually recovering the position which belongs to it, and from which first the physical struggle for existence, later race struggles, and finally political struggles in the name of imported and ill-acclimated principles had removed it. Everything, moreover, favors such an improvement: European immigration which will increase constantly, however great may be the obstacles placed in its way, for the hope of obtaining easier living conditions must always be a decoy for those who struggle with difficulties; the development of communications which will inevitably transform the desert of ignorance, albeit possessing some intellectual oases, into a fruitful and cultivated plain on which shall grow in great luxuriance the tree of knowledge, beneath whose shade certain harmful weeds which distinguished the revolutionary flora and cast the greatest discredit upon the entire continent, do not thrive.

With the increase in population, with greater facilities of communication, with all that, which, in fine, characterizes modern life will tend to disappear that comparative but real isolation in which the Latin American countries have lived with respect to one another, making difficult the interchange of ideas. The same tendencies will destroy within each of those nations that social isolation of the different classes or the different elements of the population, a situation caused by the great distances between the centers of population, by the climate, by the aspect of nature itself—steep mountains, wild forests, and swiftly-flowing streams.

The change will give place not only to a national conscience, which is still lacking, but to an American conscience, for much talking about it does not make it a reality. The national conscience will come into being as soon as the new feudalism, as Blanco Fombona calls it, the feudalism of the local *caciques,* woven in a rouph political loom, gives way to a régime of public opinion and fair elections which will remedy the lack of liberty which still characterizes some of these so-called democratic societies, and will inaugurate for all time an era of independent and fearless criticism. As the Venezuelan author already cited justly says, relief by the pen in a country enjoying a free press, frequently avoids relief by a revolution, when war is the only recourse against tyranny.

Latin America has frequently been admonished and censured as it deserves, but it has also as frequently been treated with excessive severity, and at times cruelly ridiculed and even maliciously slandered. Thus, the ignorance of the great majority of its population is not peculiar to it alone; in order to rival in this respect the more backward countries of Europe it only lacks the counterpoise of a traditional authority, strong in its military arrogance or in its administrative despotism.

Its indolence is a myth: M. Clemenceau was astonished to see how they work in Brazil, and if he made this observation about Brazil rather than Argentina or Uruguay, it was because he took into consideration the tropical climate. The distinguished French statesman expected to find the people half asleep and was greatly surprised on learning that no one even takes a siesta [34].

The so-much-talked-of wars and revolutions, which moreover are not unknown in the other continents, as the spectacle of every day proves, do not fail to show in the final analysis weighty and lofty motives; they do not come solely from a disease which has been unjustly called Iberian, or from social parasitism, by virtue of which the strong try to live at the exclusive expense of the weak.

Oppression and exploitation constitute up to a certain point the sad inheritance of a past which is far from being exclusive to us: they are features moreover which have been gradually disappearing. From the contest between the conservative and the racial tendencies, between the reactionary and the liberal forces, there has resulted here as everywhere, political and social progress, real and not apparent only.

Real and not apparent, too, is that profound, if not vast intellectual movement which is seen in Latin America and of which its conquests in the scientific, juridical and literary field are testimony.

At the Hague Conference—and I cite this in particular because it was so to speak a parliament of nations and the most important international meeting of recent times—the juridical culture of the new Spanish-Portuguese World was a revelation to many European jurists and statesmen, who did not count upon finding so much erudition, albeit disclosed in a perfectly natural manner and without betraying any effort, among a people with whom the public mind has associated the defects of intellectual negligence and revolutionary delirium.

Thus it was that we saw Brazil upholding with persuasive eloquence the juridical equality of the nations; Colombia defending the humanization of war, and Argentina go so far as to obtain that the employment of force for the collection of international debts should be condemned. Ruy Barbosa [35], Perez Triana [36], and Luiz Drago [37] were the exponents, whether of the knowledge, or of human sympathy, or of political sense, of their respective countries. And not only this; tradition exerted its influence there as usual. It was the past which once more affirmed itself in its unbroken continuity, adjoining the present.

Of Latin American scientific progress I could cite a great many instances, and would do so if it were not for your incomparable development, which necessarily makes all other achievements of the same kind appear mean by the side of them.

However, as regards Brazil, the sanitation of a city of nearly a million inhabitants like Rio de Janeiro, which is today free from the yellow fever which desolated and discredited it, constitutes a work of extraordinary scientific and social importance, and the magnificent work of the Oswaldo Cruz Laboratory [38] in connection with various endemic diseases of the country is a most creditable testimony to competence and perseverance—words which are not often employed in reference to South America, where science has been treated as bookish, literature as verbose and art as superfluous.

I am well aware that the foundation of this high state of culture is still far from being solid and adequate. The masses among us need to be educated as well as instructed. The proportion of illiterates is painfully large, in spite of the diffusion of the schools, for in this direction not a little has been done. The school system of the Argentine Republic is an honor to the country: Sarmiento was the best of the disciples of Horace Mann [39]. Rural education is being carried on successfully in Uruguay; in Chile, technical education is a reality, and in Brazil, professional education, particularly agricultural instruction, is being widely disseminated.

This is indeed the fundamental task which should occupy us; the cupola of the magnificent edifice whose foundations were laid by Columbus, Vespucius, Cabral, Cortez, Pizarro, Nuñez de Balboa, and so many other navigators and conquerors, must be the budding of the aforesaid *American conscience*.

Such a sentiment, however, cannot well harmonize, as some lightly advocate, with the establishment of a protectorate of a part of America over the other part; in order to flourish and prosper, it must strike its roots deep down in the layer where the responsibilities and rights are declared equal for all the nations of the continent.

Spanish America, in spite of its political fragmentation and the intellectual particularism of the nationalities into which it is divided, does not fail to form, up to a certain point and under different aspects, a moral whole. Among the nations comprising it, there exist, besides identity of origin, so many features of similarity, the offspring of their close relationship, that they cannot be considered isolated. They constitute a latent, or perhaps it would be better to say a spontaneous confederation, it being possible to separate them and even to set them against one another, but it is not equally possible to differentiate and integrate each one of them, for they have a common soul. The best part of Bolívar's work was his American conception; it was the dike he aimed to set up against a nationalism which had not yet been formed and only afterward was gradually organized.

The filiation and evolution of Portuguese America are separate from those of Spanish America; not infrequently, nay frequently rather, was this evolution hostile to that of Spanish America: but today they have common, identical interests, and a desire for a closer approximation appears so reciprocal that this movement becomes every day more pronounced and more firmly rooted. For Pan-Americanism to be complete, it would be necessary for the United States to ally itself with Latin America, with the importance, the influence, the prestige, the superiority to which its civilization entitles it—it would not be human to do otherwise —but without any thought, expressed or reserved, of direct predominance, which offends the weaker element and renders it suspicious [40].

It is this which those who, like myself, know and esteem the United States—and the best way of showing one's esteem is not by praising unreservedly—are hoping will come as the result of the great university movement which is gradually crystallizing in this country, where idealism is a feature of the race (nor would you without it belong to a superior race), an ideal so noble and elevated as that of respect for the rights of others, as that of human solidarity through the unification of culture. The great statesman [41] who now presides over the destinies of the Argentine Republic, proclaimed at the First Pan-American Conference, at Washington, that America belonged to all humanity, not to a fraction of it; and indeed America is and will continue to be more and more the field for the employment of European capital, of study for European scholars, of commerce for European merchants, of activity for European immigrants. Only thus will the New World fulfil its historical and social mission and redeem the debt contracted with Europe, which has given it its civilization.

NOTES ON LECTURE I.

1. GUATEMOTZIN.—Last ruler of the Aztecs. He was born about 1494 and died in 1525. After the death of his uncle Montezuma, he was elected to the position of "chief of men" by the tribal council in September, 1520. From May to August, 1521, he heroically defended Tenochtitlan, or Mexico City, against the Spaniards commanded by Cortez. On August 13, 1521, he was captured and in violation of the promise of Cortez was put to torture in the vain hope that he would reveal the hiding place of the treasures of the Aztecs. Subsequently he was forced to accompany Cortez to Honduras, but on the way was accused of treachery and hanged. He is regarded by the Mexicans as one of their national heroes, and his statue occupies a prominent place on the beautiful Alameda of Mexico City. Cf. Prescott, *Conquest of Mexico*, passim.

2. ATAHUALPA.—Inca ruler of Peru. He was the son of the Inca Huayna Capac, and was born about 1495. On the death of his father the Inca realm was divided between himself and his brother Huascar. In the quarrel which ensued between the brothers Huascar was defeated and Atahualpa's authority was acknowledged throughout the greater part of Peru. He had set out from Quito to be crowned at Cutzo when he met Pizarro and his soldiers at Caxamarca (November, 1532). Here he was treacherously seized by the Spaniards, many of his followers being massacred. Though he subsequently gathered together a ransom equal in value to fifteen million dollars, he was tried and put to death by Pizarro (August 29, 1533). Cf. Prescott, *Conquest of Peru*, book I, chs. ii-vii, and Fiske, *Discovery of America*, vol. II, ch. x.

3. Minas Geraes (lit. "General Mines").—One of the great interior states of Brazil, famous, especially during the eighteenth century, for its gold and diamond mines. The former capital, Ouro Preto (lit. "Black Gold"), is historically perhaps the most interesting city in Brazil. Area of the state, 222,160 square miles; population (estimate) 5,000,000. Statistics relative to the production of gold and silver during the colonial period are given in A. G. Keller, *Colonization*, (New York, 1908), pp. 165-167.

4. BERNAL DIAZ DEL CASTILLO.—Born in Medina del Campo about 1498; died in Nicaragua about 1593. Famous *Conquistador* and chron-

icler of the Conquest of Mexico. His work, the *Historia verdadera de la Conquista de la Nueva España*, though written in the simple unaffected style of a common soldier, remains one of the standard authorities for the conquest of Mexico. The best English edition of his work is that of A. P. Maudsley, in the Publications of the Hakluyt Society, series II, vols. XXIII-XXIV. A full discussion of the man and his work will be found in Prescott, *Conquest of Mexico*, in a long note at the end of ch. viii of book V.

5. JOSÉ MARIA DE HEREDIA (1842-1905).—A French poet and the modern master of the French sonnet. His most famous sonnets, together with a few longer poems, were published under the title of *Les Trophées* in 1893. The translation of the work of Diaz del Castillo appeared in 1881.

6. Manchineel tree.—A tree, *Hippomane Mancinella*, of moderate size, found in the West Indies, Central America and Florida. It abounds in a white, milky, poisonous sap, the virulence of which has been exaggerated. The formerly widespread belief that even the shade of the manchineel tree was of deadly effect is now relegated to the domain of legend.

7. LAS CASAS, BARTHOLOMÉ DE (1474-1566).—Known to posterity as the "Apostle of the Indies." During his long life, of which a great part was spent in America, he labored unremittingly to secure protection of the Indians against the rapacity of the Spanish conquerors. It was largely through his efforts that Indian slavery was legally abolished in Spanish America. His chief works are: *Brevissima relación de la destruyción de las Indias*, ("Destruction of the Indies," Seville, 1552), and *Historia de las Indias* (published 1875 but well known before by manuscript copies). The standard biography in English of Las Casas is that by F. A. McNutt (2 vols., New York, 1909). A remarkable appreciation of Las Casas and his work is given by Fiske in his *Discovery of America*, vol. II, ch. xi.

8. ANCHIETA, JOSÉ DE (1533-1597).—A famous Jesuit missionary, sometimes known as the "Apostle of Brazil." He was born in 1533 on the island of Teneriffe, studied at the University of Coimbra, and at the age of seventeen entered the Jesuit order. In 1553 he went as missionary to Brazil, and for the next forty-four years he labored unremittingly for the conversion and protection of the Indians. He was a scholar as well as a missionary, his *Arte de grammatica da lingua mais usada na costa do Brazil*, (Coimbra, 1595), being one of the first works on the Indian languages of Brazil. Anchieta is rightly regarded as one of the heroic figures in the history of Portuguese America.

9. PORTOCARRERO, DON MELCHOR.—Third Count of Monclova, Viceroy of Peru from 1689 to 1705. He was the last viceroy appointed during the period of the Austrian dynasty.

10. Caciques.—Originally a prince or chief among the Indians of Spanish America; later applied to the Indian officials placed over Indian villages. The term "cacique" is the Spanish form of an Haytian word meaning "chief."

11. *Ethiope resgatado.*—In 1750 a Portuguese priest, Father Manoel Ribeiro Rocha, published a work dealing with the question of negro slavery. In this work Father Rocha maintained that it is not lawful to hold negroes as merchandise, but only as a pledge (*jure pignoris*) for the performance of services equivalent to the slave's money value, on the completion of which services the slave is to be "redeemed," *i. e.*, allowed to go free. Cf. Agostinho Marques Perdigao Malheiro, *A Escravidão no Brazil*, (Rio de Janeiro, 1867), vol. II, p. 79.

12. POMBAL, SEBASTIÃO JOSÉ CARVALLIO DE MELLO, Marquis of (1699-1782).—The famous reforming minister of King Joseph I of Portugal. The effect of his sweeping changes and reforms was not confined to Portugal. As regards Brazil he not only expelled the Jesuits but curbed the power of other religious establishments, alleviated the lot of the Jews, liberated the Indians, and promoted industry and commerce. On this subject cf. R. G. Watson, *Spanish and Portuguese South America during the Colonial Period*, (London, 1884), vol. II, pp. 238-239.

13. FERDINAND VII of Spain.—Held "prisoner" by Napoleon in the castle of Valençay from 1808 to 1814. During the Spanish American Wars of Independence many of the revolutionists employed their loudly proclaimed loyalty to Ferdinand VII as a convenient pretext for overthrowing the vice-regal authority.

14. LABOULAYE, EDWARD RENÉ LEFÈBVRE DE (1811-1883).—The well known French jurist, historian and politician. The statement referred to by Dr. Lima is found in his *Histoire politique des Etats Unis*, (Paris, 1855-1866).

15. Araucanians.—A tribal group of Indians inhabiting portions of Chile south of the Bio-Bio river. They are the most tough-fibred and warlike of all the South American Indians. They were never conquered by the Incas, long offered effective resistance to the Spaniards of colonial Chile, and have been only partially assimilated by the Chilians of today. The so called "rotos," who form the bulk of the lower classes of Chile, are of mixed Spanish and Araucanian stock. An illuminating discussion

of the peculiar political formation of modern Chile may be found in the article by Professor P. S. Reinsch entitled "Parliamentary Government in Chile," in the *American Political Science Review*, vol. III, pp. 507-539, (1909).

16. Battle of Carabobo.—A decisive battle fought on June 27, 1821, between Bolívar and the Spanish General La Torre, resulting in the independence of northwestern South America. On this occasion the nine hundred Englishmen comprising the British Legion played an important part. An interesting account of this battle, with a description of its site, is given by Professor Hiram Bingham in the appendix to his work *Diary of an Expedition across Venezuela and Colombia*, (New Haven, 1909).

17. In the expression "from Ávila to Potosí," the Ávila referred to is not, of course, the city of Spain of this name, but a mountain called Ávila rising above Caracas, the capital of Venezuela. Potosí is the well known mining center of Bolivia.

18. JUAN and ULLOA.—An interesting analysis of those portions of the "Noticias Secretas" which deal with the abuses practiced by the Spanish authorities on the Indians is given in chapter viii of Professor Bernard Moses' *South America on the Eve of Emancipation*, (New York and London, 1908). In addition to their secret report in the Indies, (published in English in London in 1826), Juan and Ulloa published *Relación histórica del viaje á la America meridional* (2 vols. 1748: the English in Pinkerton's Travels, vol. IV) ; and Juan alone, *Noticias americanas* (1772).

19. LA CONDAMINE, CHARLES MARIE DE (1701-1774).—In company with Godin and Bouguer this noted French scientist conducted an expedition to South America in 1735 to measure an arc of the meridian on the plane of Quito. He subsequently separated from the rest of his party and undertook the first scientific exploration of the Amazon. His most important work dealing with South America is his *Relation abrégée d'un voyage fait dans l'intérieur de l'Amérique méridionale*, (Paris, 1745). He is said to have carried the first knowledge of India rubber to Europe.

20. CHARLES III.—King of Spain from 1759 to 1788. He was the most enlightened and progressive ruler of the Spanish branch of the Bourbon family, and was responsible for many reforms both in Spain and Spanish America. The standard biography of Charles III is that of M. F. Rousseau, *Le Règne de Carlos III d'Espagne*, (2 vols., Paris, 1907).

21. DEPONS, FRANÇOIS RAYMOND JOSEPH DE.—*Voyage à la partie orientale de la Terre Ferme dans l'Amérique Méridionale fait pendant*

les années 1801-1804, (Paris, 1806). An English translation of this work (attributed to Washington Irving) appeared in New York in 1806.

22. These lectures of Señor Rufino Blanco Fombona were given in Madrid under the auspices of the Unión Ibero-America, on June 16 and 23, 1911. They were published at Madrid the same year under the title, *La Evolución politica y social de Hispano-America.*

23. JUAREZ, BENITO (1806-1872).—The famous Mexican statesman and patriot, president of the republic during the critical period from 1858 to 1871. Juarez' two great triumphs were his victory over the clerical and reactionary party, resulting in the ultra-liberal constitution of 1859, and the overthrow of the empire of Maximilian supported by Napoleon III. The most satisfactory biography of Juarez is that by U. R. Burke, *Life of Benito Juarez,* (London, 1907).

24. ALTAMIRANO, IGNACIO MANUEL (1835-1893).—A Mexican poet, orator and statesman, of pure Aztec blood, said to have been a descendant of the Aztec rulers of Mexico. He participated in the War of Reform, aided President Juarez during the French Intervention, and was a partner in the glory of the reëstablished republic. Subsequently he represented Mexico in Europe, being at various times Consul-General to both Spain and France. Of his numerous literary productions the most famous is perhaps his *Paisajes y Leyandas,* (Mexico, 1884). A brief biography of Altamirano, with English translations of excerpts from his writings, may be found in Professor Frederick Starr's *Readings from Modern Mexican Authors,* (Chicago, 1904).

25. HOMAIS.—In this character Flaubert has portrayed with consummate skill the type of village apothecary whose naïve provincialism is equalled only by his rabid anti-clericalism.

26. Carbonario regicide.—The reference here is of course to the secret society of radical republicans who were in part responsible for the assassination of King Carlos of Portugal in 1908. Later the "Carbonarios" were instrumental in bringing about the overthrow of the monarchy, and at the present time are charged with exercising an undue influence in the affairs of the Portuguese Republic.

27. Cf. *O Congresso Universal das Raças Apreciacões e Commentarios* pel Dr. J. B. de Lacerda, (Rio de Janeiro, 1911).

28. Guipuzcoa Company.—A brief, but excellent account of the activity of the *Compañia Guipuzcoana* is given in Professor Bernard Moses' *Establishment of Spanish Rule in America.* (New York, 1898), pp. 166-171.

29. VIEIRA, ANTONIO.—Born at Lisbon in 1608; died at Bahia, Bra-

zil, in 1697. A celebrated Portuguese missionary, pulpit orator, author and publicist. He was taken to Bahia as a child, and entered the Jesuit order there in 1625. As a preacher he soon became famous for his eloquence; after his return to Portugal, in 1641, he was loaded with honors by King John IV, being intrusted with important diplomatic missions to Paris, The Hague and Rome. In 1652 he was placed in charge of the Jesuit missions at Maranhão, and soon drew upon himself the hatred of the slave-owning colonists through his efforts to protect the Indians. From then on he became the champion of the oppressed Indians, pleading their cause both in Brazil and Portugal with a courage and fervor worthy of Las Casas. Vieira was not only interested in the spiritual and economic welfare of Brazil, but in Portuguese letters as well, and his many literary productions entitle him to a place among the peers of Brazilian prose writers. An account of Vieira's activities in Brazil and Portugal may be found in Watson, *Spanish and Portuguese South America during the Colonial Period*, (London, 1884), and in Southey, *History of Brazil*, (3 vols., London, 1822).

30. An account of the Pará-Maranhão Company is given in Watson, II, pp. 238-239.

31. Dr. Lima here refers to the seventeenth Congress of Americanists, which met at Buenos Aires in May, 1910. Of Señor Quesada's literary productions the best known are: *El Vireinato del Rio de la Plata, 1776-1810*, (Buenos Aires); *Recuerdos de mi vida diplomatica*, (Buenos Aires); *Mis memorias diplomaticas*, (Buenos Aires).

32. See note following.

33. NARIÑO, ANTONIO (1765-1823).— A New-Granadan patriot. Though he held important offices under the Spanish viceroys, he was an ardent champion of Spanish American independence, and in 1795 published at Bogota a Spanish translation of the *Droits des hommes*. For this he was imprisoned, and did not obtain his release until 1810. On the outbreak of the Revolution he played a conspicuous part in the liberation of New Granada from Spain, but was captured by the Royalists in 1814, and was confined as a prisoner in Spain until 1820. After his return to New Granada he was elected vice-president and senator of the republic.

34. The Jesuit Order was expelled from Portugal in 1759.

NOTES ON LECTURE II.

1. The Plateau of Cundinamarca occupies a portion of the eastern central part of the Republic of Colombia. It was formerly the seat of the civilization of the Chibchas; at the present time the name is applied to the department having Bogotá as its capital.

2. GAMA, JOSÉ BASILIO DA.—Born at San José, Minas Geraes, 1740; died at Lisbon, 1795. One of the most celebrated of the poets of Colonial Brazil. He was a novice of the Jesuits, leaving that order upon its expulsion from Brazil. After traveling extensively in Europe he made his home in Lisbon. His epic poem *O Uruguay* was published in 1769.

3. GUSMÃO, ALEXANDRE.—Born in Santos, Brazil, 1695; died at Lisbon, 1753. Though a Brazilian by birth, Alexandre Gusmão rose to a position of great eminence in Portugal, being justly considered one of the foremost Portuguese statesmen of the period. After obtaining his doctorate at Paris he was sent to Rome on an important diplomatic mission by John V. It was largely through his efforts that the Portuguese king obtained from the pope the title of "Fedelissimo" (Most Faithful). As a diplomatist Gusmão's consummate skill is seen in the protracted negotiations between Portugal and Spain, culminating in the Treaty of 1750. This treaty fixed the boundaries between Spanish and Portuguese America on the basis of *uti possidetes;* it was considered a diplomatic triumph for Portugal. A full account of Gusmão's diplomatic and literary activities is given in J. M. Pereira da Silva, *Os Varões illustres do Brazil durante os Tempos coloniaes*, (Paris, 1858), vol. I, pp. 229-256.

4. DOM JOHN V.—King of Portugal, 1706-1750. The absurdities in the court of this ruler largely sprang from a ridiculous desire to imitate Louis XIV, a fondness for empty titles, and extravagance in squandering vast sums on buildings, especially on the great convent at Mafra (said to have cost over $20,000,000). Cf. H. Morse Stephens, *History of Portugal*, pp. 350 *et seq.*

5. Coimbra.—The seat of the only university in Portugal. It was founded in 1290 in Lisbon and transferred to Coimbra in 1308.

6. MIRANDA, FRANCISCO ANTONIO GABRIEL DE.—Born at Caracas, Venezuela, 1756; died at Cadiz, Spain, July 1816. During his adventurous career in England, Miranda was busy plotting for the emancipation

of Spanish South America, and in 1806 he made an unsuccessful attempt to lead a revolt in Venezuela. On the breaking out of the Revolution two years later he returned to Venezuela, and became dictator in 1812. But in the same year, partly as a result of a severe earthquake which was interpreted as a sign of divine displeasure at the revolution, the Royalists gained the upper hand, and Miranda was forced to surrender. He was sent to Spain, and died in prison at Cadiz four years later. The standard biography of Miranda is that of W. S. Robertson, *Francisco de Miranda*, in the Annual Report of the American Historical Association, I, 266 *et seq.*

7. For a brief account of this revolt see T. C. Dawson, *The South American Republics*, (New York, 1910), I, pp. 409-410.

8. Dr. Lima here refers, of course, to the transference of the Portuguese court and center of government from Lisbon to Brazil in 1808.

9. GONÇALVES DIAS, ANTONIO.—Born at Caxias, Maranhão, 1824; died at sea, 1864. The foremost of Brazilian poets. After taking his degree at the University of Coimbra he was appointed professor of history at the Collegio Dom Pedro II at Rio de Janeiro. He was subsequently employed in various literary commissions in northern Brazil and in Europe, meanwhile gaining a national reputation as a dramatist and above all as a lyric poet. Owing to failing health he sought a change of climate in Europe; on his return in 1864 he perished by shipwreck in sight of his native shore. His works include *Primeiros cantos* (1846); *Segundos cantos e sextilhas de Frei Antão* (1848); and *Ultimos cantos* (1851).

10. The *Recopolación de leyes de los reynos de las Indias*, (last edition, 4 vols., Madrid, 1841).

11. ZUMÁRRAGA, JUAN DE.—Born near Durango, Biscay, 1486; died at Mexico City, 1548. The first bishop of Mexico. He arrived in Mexico in 1527 and immediately became the zealous champion of the native population, receiving the title and office of Protector of the Indians. Through his efforts various schools for the Indians were founded and missionary activity extended throughout large portions of Mexico and Spanish America. At the same time he gained a melancholy renown for the wholesale destruction of all Aztec manuscripts on which he could lay hands, and at his instance similar scenes were enacted in other towns and cities of New Spain. He was raised to the position of Archbishop of Mexico eight days before his death. See Joaquin Garcia Icazbalceta *Don Fray Juan Zumarraga, primero obispo y arzobispo de Mexico*, (Mexico, 1896), *Obras*, I.

12. MENDOZA, ANTONIO DE (1485-1552) —The first viceroy of New Spain, which office he held from 1535 to 1549. A full account of his activities in Mexico may be found in Bancroft, *History of Mexico*, (San Francisco, 1877), vol. II, pp. 375-385.

13. POPE ALEXANDER VI by his famous Papal Bull of May 3, 1493, drew a line of demarcation "one hundred leagues west of the Azores and Cape Verde Islands," giving to Spain the right of conquest to the west of it, and to Portugal the same right on the east. The Convention of Tordesillas, signed by representatives of Spain and Portugal at the Spanish town of Tordesillas on June 7, 1494, removed the line of demarcation to a meridian 370 leagues west of the Cape Verde Islands, thus, as it later proved, putting Brazil within the sphere of the Portuguese. Cf. on this subject Fiske, *Discovery of America*, (Boston, 1892), I, ch. vi.

14. CASTILLO DE BOBADILLA, *Politica para corregidores y señores de vasallos en tiempo de paz y guerra y para prelados en lo espiritual y temporal entre legos, iuezes de commissión . . . y otros oficiales publicos. Autor el licenciado Castillo de Bobadilla*, (2 vols., Medino del Campo, 1608.)

15. Revolt of the Communeros.—The famous revolt of the Castilian Communes against the tyranny of Emperor Charles V (Carlos I of Spain). The revolt broke out in 1519 and was finally suppressed in 1521, after the decisive defeat of the Communeros at the Battle of Villalar (April 1521). Cf. Armstrong, *Emperor Charles V*, (New York, 1902), I, ch. v.

16. CÁNOVAS DEL CASTILLO, ANTONIO (1828-1897).—A Spanish statesman and leader of the Conservative Party. He was largely instrumental in securing the restoration of the Bourbons in the person of Alfonso XII. Between 1875 and 1897 he was five times premier, his career finally being cut short by the bullet of an anarchist in August, 1897. His writings include *Historia general de España* (a coöperative work of which he was editor), (Madrid, 1891 fol.), and *Estudios del reinado de Filipe IV*, (2 vols., Madrid, 1880).

17. For a qualified approval of this system of selling public offices in the *cabildos* see Bourne, *Spain in America*, (New York, 1904), pp. 237-239. The system is unsparingly condemned by the Argentine author J. Garcia in his *Ciudad indiana*, (Buenos Aires, 1910), pp. 169-170.

18. Reference here is made to a paper read by Dr. Salgado on the *cabildo* at the Congress of Americanists held at Buenos Aires in 1910.

19. MITRE, BARTOLOMÉ.—Born at Buenos Aires, 1821; died there, 1894. A famous Argentine general, statesman and writer. After an

active participation in the political life of Argentina he was elected president for the period 1862-1868, fulfilling the duties of his office with great ability. He subsequently occupied important diplomatic positions, including that of minister to Brazil. In 1852 he founded "La Nación," which soon became the most important journal of Buenos Aires, and which remained under his direction until his death. Besides a large number of poems, essays, speeches, etc. he published two important historical works, the *Historia de Belgrano* (1857 et seq.), and *Historia de San Martin* (1884, English abridged translation, 1893).

20. The standard histories which cover wholly or part of this critical period in Brazilian history are Oliveira Lima, *Dom João VI no Brazil*, (2 vols., Rio de Janeiro, 1911), and Pereira da Silva, *Historia da fundacão do imperio brazileiro*, (7 vols., Rio de Janeiro, 1864-1868). Cf. also Dawson, *South American Republics*, (New York, 1904), vol. I, and Armitage, *History of Brazil*, (2 vols., London, 1836).

21. Dom Pedro (Dom Antonio Pedro da Alcantara Bourbon).—Born in Lisbon, 1788; died there, 1834. Second son of King John VI, whom he accompanied to Brazil in 1808. Upon the return of John VI to Brazil in 1821, Dom Pedro was left as regent. On September 7, 1822, Dom Pedro pronounced for independence from Portugal; on October 12 he was proclaimed emperor, under title of Dom Pedro I, being crowned December 1. On April 7, 1831, he abdicated in favor of his son, later famous as Emperor Dom Pedro II. For references to authorities see preceding note.

22. Ricardo Palma (d. 1913).—Author of *Tradiciones del Peru*, (4 vols., Barcelona, 1893). Well known to all investigators of Latin American history as the distinguished and scholarly director of the National Library at Lima.

23. Don Vicente Quesada.—See Lecture I, note 31.

24. Juan and Ulloa.—See Lecture I, note 18.

NOTES ON LECTURE III.

1. HANDELMANN, HEINRICH, *Geschichte von Brasilien*, (Berlin, 1860).
2. SOUTHEY, ROBERT, *History of Brazil*, (3 vols., London, 1810-1819).
3. PI Y MARGALL.—The reference here is probably to *Les Nationalités*, (Paris, 1879).
4. COELHO DA ROCHA, M. A., *Ensaio sobre a historia do governo e da legistação de Portugal para servir de introducção do estudo do direito patrio*, (3d edition, Coimbra, 1851).
5. DIEGO DO CONTO, *Observacaões sobre as principaes causas da decadencia dos Portuguezes na Asia com o titulo de soldado pratico*, (Lisboa, 1790).
6. *Op. cit.*, pp. 87-88.
7. Audiencias.—For an able discussion of this institution cf. Moses, *Establishment of Spanish Rule in America*, ch. iv.
8. ARANDA, COUNT OF, (PEDRO PABLO ABARCA Y BOLEA, 1718-1799).—A Spanish statesman and diplomatist, celebrated as one of the reforming ministers of Charles III.
9. This whole episode, including an account of the interview between Maia and Thomas Jefferson in the amphitheater of Nimes, is given by Dr. Lima in his *Formation historique de la nationalité brésilienne*, (Paris, 1911), pp. 115-116.
10. See note 16 to Lecture I.
11. For a brief but excellent discussion of this critical period of Brazilian History cf. Dawson, vol. I, chs. xiii-xvi.
12. VILLANUEVA, CARLOS A., *La monarquía en America*, (2 vols., Paris, 1911).

   VILLANUEVA, *op. cit.*, tomo I, *secunda parte*.
13. COCHRANE, THOMAS, Tenth Earl of Dundonald (1775-1860).—A British naval commander famous for his participation in the Spanish American Wars of Independence. In 1818 he accepted an invitation to organize the infant navy of Chile, and as admiral of the Chilian fleet practically annihilated the Spanish sea power in the South Pacific. In 1820 he transported the army of San Martin from Valparaiso to Callao and greatly facilitated the capture of Lima. Owing to quarrels with

the Spanish American Revolutionists he left their service and assumed command of the Brazilian Navy; in this new capacity he recovered Bahia and Maranhão from the Portuguese. A detailed account of his activities during his stirring period is given in *The Life of Thomas, Lord Cochrane* by his son, Thomas, Eleventh Earl of Dundonald, (2 vols., London, 1869).

14. MILLER, WILLIAM.—Born in Wingham, Kent, December 2, 1795; died at Callao, Peru, October 31, 1861. An English general in the service of Peru. After engaging in the War of 1812 between the United States and Great Britain, he took service with the Revolutionists at Buenos Aires in 1816; subsequently he held independent commands in Chile and Peru, and played an important part in the decisive battles of Junin and Ayacucho (1824). His Memoirs, published by his brother, John Miller, in 1829, form one of the best authorities on the Spanish American Revolution.

15. Reference to this fantastic proposal may be found in Villanueva, *op. cit.*, t. I, *secunda parte*. Tupac Amaru, sometimes called the "Last of the Incas," was a Peruvian revolutionist, said to be a direct descendant of the early Incas. In 1780 he led the Indians of Peru in a rebellion against the Spanish authorities. After a number of minor successes the rebellion was put down with great cruelty, while Tupac Amaru was executed after suffering horrible tortures. This rebellion was the most formidable in the colonial history of Spanish America, and indirectly paved the way for the Wars of Independence. An excellent account of the rebellion of Tupac Amaru is given in Moses, *South America on the Eve of Emancipation*, ch. viii.

16. By "Indianism" Dr. Lima of course refers to that somewhat fantastic idealization of Indian life and customs reflected in the poems and romances of the Brazilian authors, Gonçalves Dias and José de Alencar.

17. BELGRANO, MANUEL (1770-1820).—An Argentine general prominent in the earlier period of the Spanish American Wars of Independence; he was superceded in command of the revolutionary forces by San Martin in 1816. His life has been made the subject of a detailed study by the Argentine statesman and writer, Bartolemé Mitre, *Historia de Belgrano*, (Buenos Aires, 1857, *et seq.*).

18. RIVADAVIA, BERNADINO (1780-1845).—An Argentine statesman. Between 1811 and 1827 he occupied many public positions of great importance and influence, including that of President of the Argentine Confederation; in the formative period of the Argentine Republic he was a commanding figure. According to Mitre "he stands in America second alone to Washington as the representative statesman of a free people."

19. PUEYRREDON, JUAN MARTIN (1780-1845).—An Argentine gen-

eral and statesman. He was "Supreme Dictator" of the United Provinces of La Plata during the critical years 1816-1819. It was largely through his efforts that San Martin was able to organize the "Army of the Andes" which liberated Chile from the control of Spain. A detailed account of the activities of Pueyrredon and Rivadavia during this period is given by Mitre in his *Historia de San Martin* (1884; English abridged translation by E. Pilling, 1893).

20. DUKE OF LUCCA.—The diplomatic negotiations centering about the Duke of Lucca are discussed by Villanueva, *op. cit.*, I, pp. 131-164.

21. LA SERNA Y HINOJOSA, JOSÉ DE (1770-1832).—The last viceroy of Peru. He was defeated by General Sucre and his whole army captured at the battle of Ayacucho, December 9, 1824, thus virtually bringing to an end Spanish rule in South America.

22. PEZUELA, JOAQUIN DE LA (1761-1830).—Viceroy of Peru from 1816 to 1821. Owing to his failure to make headway against the revolutionists he was deposed by his officers January 29, 1821, and soon after returned to Spain. For an account of events in Peru at this period see the *History of Peru* by Sir Clements R. Markham, (Chicago, 1812).

23. APODACA, JUAN RUIZ DE (1754-1835).—Viceroy of New Spain from 1816 to 1822. Though an able administrator he could not put down the revolution headed by Iturbide, and was virtually forced to abdicate.

24. O'DONOJU, JUAN (1755-1821).—The last Spanish ruler in New Spain. In 1821 he was appointed captain general and acting viceroy of New Spain, but on reaching Vera Cruz discovered that the revolution had gained such strength that he was forced to temporize. On August 24, 1821, he signed with Iturbide the Treaty of Córdoba, practically surrendering Mexico to the revolutionists. A full account of conditions in Mexico at this period is given in Bancroft, *History of Mexico*, vol. III, *passim*.

25. Trocadero.—The name given to a fort near Cadiz captured by the French from the Spanish revolutionists, August 31, 1823. The square in Paris containing the Exposition building in 1878 was named after this "victory."

26. ITURBIDE.—For further details regarding this ill-starred Mexican emperor cf. Bancroft, *op. cit.*, III, ch. xx.

27. Interview of Guayaquil.—Probably the best discussion yet written of this baffling subject is that of Villanueva, *op. cit.*, I, 199-283.

28. Cf. Villanueva, *ibid*.

29. A summary of this dispatch of the Colombian envoy Zea is given by Villanueva, *op. cit.*, I, 198.

30. O'HIGGINS, BERNARDO (1776-1842).—A celebrated Chilian general and statesman. He was the son of the famous Viceroy Ambrosio O'Higgins. While studying in England he gained revolutionary ideas from Miranda, and at the outbreak of the Wars of Independence he became a leader of the Chilian patriots. Defeated at Rancagua in 1814 he joined San Martin in the invasion of Chile and had a decisive part in the victory of Chacabuco (February 12, 1817). He was subsequently chosen "Supreme Director of Chile" with dictatorial powers, but a revolution fomented by his enemies forced him into exile in 1823. He is the most notable figure in the liberation of Chile. Perhaps the best account of O'Higgins' activity at this time is found in Diego Barros Arana's *Historia general de la independencia de Chile*, (4 vols., Santiago, 1854-58; Paris, 1856).

31. The most important of these revolts was that of Tupac Amaru. Cf. note 15 to this Lecture.

32. ALTAMIRA, RAPHAEL.—The distinguished professor of history at the University of Oviedo. The most important of his many works is his *Historia de España e de la civilización española*, (4 vols., Barcelona, 1900-1911).

33. For a brief account of the activities of the Visitador-general José Galvez cf. Bancroft, *History of Mexico*, III, ch. xx, and Don E. Smith, *The Viceroy of New Spain in the Eighteenth Century*, in the Annual Report of the American Historical Association, 1908, vol. I, pp. 171-181.

34. An excellent account of the attempts of Sir Home Popham and Brigadier-General Beresford to gain possession of Buenos Aires is given by Professor Bernard Moses in his *South America on the Eve of Emancipation*, chs. xi and xii.

35. LINIERS Y BRÉMONT, SANTIAGO ANTONIO MARIA DE (1756-1810). —A French royal officer in the Spanish naval service. It was largely through his efforts that the English were definitely expelled from the La Plata region in 1808. On the outbreak of the Wars of Independence he attempted to reëstablish the royal authority, but was captured and shot. The standard biography of Liniers is that of Paul Groussac, *Santiago de Liniers, Conde de Buenos Aires, 1753-1810*, (Buenos Aires, 1907).

36. The Cadiz Regency, consisting of five members, attempted to rule Spain in the name of the exiled Ferdinand VII from January 31 to September 24, 1810. Its most important act was the summoning of the famous Cortes of Cadiz to which the American Colonies were invited to send representatives. Cf. Martin Hume, *Modern Spain*, (London, 1899), pp. 165 *et seq*.

NOTES ON LECTURE IV.

1. HIDALGO Y COSTILLA, MIGUEL (1753-1811).—The first leader of the Mexican Wars of Independence. While curate of the village of Dolores he raised the standard of revolt ("Grito de Dolores"). After several minor successes he was disastrously defeated by Calleja at the bridge of Calderon, January 17, 1811. In attempting to escape to the United States he was captured, tried, and on August 1, 1811, was executed at Chihuahua. Cf. Bancroft, *History of Mexico*, III, passim; Noll and McMahon, *The Life and Times of Miguel Hidalgo y Costilla*, (Chicago, 1910).

2. MORELOS Y PAVON (1765-1815).—A Mexican priest prominent in the earlier period of the Wars of Independence. He took up the work of Hidalgo; for a time was very successful, but after 1813 met a crushing series of defeats. On November 15, 1815, he was captured, tried by the Inquisition, and executed December 22, 1815. He was probably the last victim of the Holy Office in New Spain. Cf. Prescott, *Conquest of Mexico*, III, *passim*.

3. An excellent account of conditions in Pernambuco at this period is given by Dr. Lima in his *Pernambuco, seu desenvolvimento historico*, (Leipzig, 1895). Cf. also notes 12 and 13 to this Lecture.

4. FEIJO, DIEGO ANTONIO (1784-1843).—A Brazilian priest, prominent in History of Brazil from 1822 to 1837. In 1822 he was sent as a representative from the province of São Paulo to the famous Portuguese Cortes of that year. He made an eloquent speech in defence of Brazilian rights, which were threatened by the Portuguese majority. On his return to Brazil he was elected by the province of São Paulo to the legislatures of 1826-1829 and 1830-1833. In 1827 he proposed the abolition of clerical celibacy, and in the following year submitted a project for the reform of municipalities. During the stormy period from 1833 to 1837 he was one of the foremost men of the empire, being elected regent of Brazil in 1834. In his new office he proclaimd a liberal and advanced program, but he encountered such opposition that he resigned his office September 18, 1837, retiring shortly afterwards to private life. Cf. Eugenio Egas, *Diego Feijo*, (2 vols., São Paulo, 1912).

5. NABUCO, JOAQUIM (1849-1910).—A distinguished Brazilian diplomatist and author. He was a member of the Brazilian Parliament during

the Empire, took an active part in the abolition of slavery during the years 1879-1888, and after the proclamation of the Republic fulfilled with great credit a number of high diplomatic positions. He was appointed ambassador to Washington in 1905 when Brazil created in the United States her first embassy. This important post he held until his death in 1910.

Dr. Nabuco was the author of a number of works of great literary and historical value. Among these are *O Abolicionismo*, (London, 1883), an impassioned plea for immediate negro emancipation; *Minha Formacão*, (Paris, 1910), a delightful autography; and finally, *Um estadista do imperio*, (3 vols., Paris, 1897), a scholarly monograph on the life and times of his father, Nabuco de Araujo.

6. Syllabus.—The famous "Syllabus errorium" issued by Pope Pius IX in 1864. It is a wholesale condemnation of liberalism, both in state and church.

7. The last struggle between church and state in Brazil was the famous "Affair of Olinda," which occurred in 1872-1875. It was an unsuccessful attempt on the part of certain members of the higher clergy of Brazil, especially the Bishop of Olinda, to eliminate from the Church and from the benevolent brotherhoods or *Irmandades* the influence of the Masonic Order. Cf. Nabuco, *Um estadista do imperio*, vol. III; J. Bournichon, S.J., *Le Brésil d'aujourdui*, (Paris, 1910), ch. ix.

8. See above, note 1.

9. Dr. Lima refers more specifically to the alliance of the higher Mexican clergy with certain prominent revolutionists, especially Iturbide and Guerrero. The result of this alliance was the "Plan of Iguala," which not only provided for complete independence from Spain but also specifically safeguarded the rights and property of the Church. Cf. Bancroft, *History of Mexico*, vol. III, *passim*.

10. LABRA, RAPHAEL M. DE (1841-).—A distinguished Spanish writer and educator. Though born in Cuba, at the age of ten he was taken by his parents to Madrid, where he was educated and admitted to the bar in 1860. He took an active part in the movement for the abolition of slavery in the Spanish colonies, and in 1869 was elected president of the first anti-slavery society ever established in Spain. In 1871 he was elected a member of the Cortes by Porto Rico, and up to the Spanish American War he constantly represented, as a pronounced liberal, either Cuba or Porto Rico. At the same time he fulfilled the duties of professor in the University of Madrid, and wrote numerous books and articles, generally of a historical character. These include *La cuestión colonial* (1868);

La colonisación en la historia (1877); *La abolición de la esclavitúd* (1882), etc.

11. AYACUCHO, BATTLE OF.—The most memorable and decisive battle in the Spanish American Wars of Independence was won by General Sucre, December 9, 1824, at Ayacucho, midway between Lima and Cuzco. The Viceroy Serna, the commander of the Spanish forces, was taken prisoner, and the independence of Spanish America was assured.

12. RIBEIROS.—Joao Ribeiro Pessoa de Mello Montenegro, known as Padre Ribeiro. A liberal priest implicated in the ill-starred Revolution of 1817. This uprising was due to the Brazilians' jealousy of the Portuguese, and the examples of the French and American revolutions. It was put down with great cruelty by the royal government. When the rebellion collapsed Ribeiro committed suicide rather than fall in the hands of the royalists (May 20, 1817). Cf. *Compendio de historia do Brazil*, pelo P. Raphael M. Galanti, S.J., (São Paulo, 1905), t. IV, pp. 48-69; Pereira da Silva, *Historia da fundacão do imperio brazileiro*, t. IV.

13. ROMA.—José Ignacio Ribeiro de Abreu e Lima, known as "Padre Roma." Like Ribeiro, Roma was an enthusiastic leader of the Revolution of 1817. Sent on a special mission to arouse a revolt in the provinces of Alagoas and Bahia, he was captured by the Portuguese commander Conde dos Arcos and shot as a traitor. For references see preceding note.

14. Junin, Battle of (August 6, 1824).—In this engagement Bolívar defeated the royalists under Canterac. The battles of Junin and Ayacucho, by crushing the remaining Spanish power in Upper Peru, brought the Wars of Independence to an end.

15. *Cabildo abierto*.—For an excellent discussion of the part played by the *cabildo* in the history of Spanish America see Moses, *South America on the Eve of Emancipation*, ch. iv, ("The Colonial City").

16. For an account of events in Venezuela in 1810 cf. Dawson, *South American Republics*, I, 356-383; and Manchini, *Bolívar et l'émancipation des colonies espagnoles*, (Paris, 1912).

17. Para-Maranhão State.—The State of Maranhão was established by royal decree of June 3, 1621; it included the former captaincies of Maranhão, Ceará, and Pará. The first governor was appointed in 1624, although he did not take formal possession until two years later. In 1733 the seat of government was transferred from São Luiz to Pará, and in 1772 the separate state was abolished. Cf. J. P. Oliveira Martins, *O Brazil e as colonias portuguezas*, (Lisboa, 1904), p. 60.

18. José Bonifacio (José Bonifacio de Andrade e Silva), (1765-1838).—A celebrated Brazilian statesman and scholar. Though born in Santos, Brazil, José Bonifacio completed his studies in Europe. Under the patronage of the Lisbon Royal Academy he travelled extensively, studying mineralogy and metallurgy under the most famous teachers of the time. In 1800 he was appointed professor of metallurgy at the University of Coimbra, and in 1812 was made perpetual secretary of the Lisbon academy of sciences. He returned to Brazil in 1819 and at once became an ardent supporter of national independence. Entering politics he was made minister of the interior and foreign affairs in 1822, and it was on his advice that Dom Pedro threw off allegiance to Portugal. He soon fell out with the emperor, however, and owing to his bitter opposition in the Constituent Assembly was banished to France (1823), living in Bordeaux till 1829, when he returned to Brazil. During the minority of Dom Pedro II he was chosen as the young prince's guardian and tutor. In 1833 he was tried on a charge of intriguing for the return of Dom Pedro I, was acquitted, but deprived of his place. The best account of the activity and influence of José Bonifacio is probably that given by Pereira da Silva in his *Os varões illustres do Brazil durante os tempos coloniaes*, (Paris, 1858), tomo II, pp. 249-299.

19. Pichincha and Maypu.—Two important battles in the War of Independence. In the slope of the volcano Pichincha in Ecuador, General Sucre on May 24, 1822, overwhelmingly defeated the royalists under Ramirez, thus freeing Ecuador from Spanish rule. The battleground is 15,000 feet above sea level, probably the highest battlefield in the world. In the Battle of Maypu, some seven miles from Santiago de Chile, General San Martin on April 5, 1818, defeated the Spaniards under Osorio. This victory, one of the immediate results of San Martin's spectacular passage of the Andes, practically secured the independence of Chile.

20. Garcia Calderon, Francisco Maria.—A Peruvian sociologist and historian, the son of the Peruvian statesman, Francisco Garcia Calderon (1834-). His chief works are *Le Pérou contemporain* (Paris, 1907), and *Les démocraties latines de l'Amérique*, (Paris, 1912; English translation, London and New York, 1913).

21. San Martin went into exile in 1823 and save for a brief period remained in France until his death. For a time he lived near Paris in great poverty on the proceeds of the sale of a house given him by the Argentine Congress after the Battle of Maypu. In 1832 the Spanish banker Aguada, who had been one of his comrades in the Peninsular War, came to his assistance. He gave him a small country house on the banks of the

Seine, and here, surrounded by trees and flowers, he passed the remaining years of his life. His chief occupation was the care and education of his daughter, who had shared with him all the hardships of exile. Cf. Mitre, *Life of San Martin*, (Pilling's trans.), p. 473 *et seq.*

22. Baylen, Capitulation of.—By this capitulation the French general Dupont and his army surrendered to the Spaniards under General Castaños (July 22, 1808). It was the first important success won by the Spaniards over the French in the Napoleonic Wars.

Tudela.—A town in Northern Spain, in the province of Navarre. Near here in 1808 the Spanish forces under Generals Castaños and Palafox were twice defeated by the French under Marshal Lannes.

23. Boyacá, Battle of.—On August 7, 1819, Bolívar defeated the royalists under Barreiro at the village of Boyacá in Colombia. This victory practically secured the independence of Colombia or New Granada.

24. For the Battle of Junin see above, note 14.

25. A full account of the Congress of Panama is given in the *Reports* of the First International American Conference, Historical appendix, (Washington, 1890).

26. On this whole subject see W. S. Robertson, *Francisco de Miranda*, chs. xiii-xiv. Cf. also note 6 to Lecture II.

27. DRAGO.—See below, Lecture VI, note 34.

28. RIVADAVIA.—See above, Lecture III, note 18.

29. BELGRANO.—See above, Lecture III, note 17.

30. O'HIGGINS.—See above, Lecture III, note 30.

31. SUCRE, ANTONIO JOSÉ DE.—Born at Cumaná, Venezuela, 1793, died in New Granada, 1830. A famous general of the Spanish American Wars of Independence. By his victory at Pichincha (May 24, 1822) he liberated Quito or Ecuador, and by his victory at Ayacucho (December 9, 1824), completed the independence of Spanish South America. He was elected president of Bolivia in 1826 and subsequently fought in the war between Colombia and Peru on the side of Colombia. The city of Sucre, the official capital of Bolivia, is named after him.

32. DOM PEDRO I.—See Lecture II, note 21.

33. JOSÉ BONIFACIO.—See above, note 18.

34. PAEZ, JOSÉ ANTONIO (1790-1873).—A Venezuelan general and politician. Together with Bolívar he played a prominent part in the liberation of Venezuela from Spain; subsequently under the Republic of Greater Colombia he was made supreme military commander in Venezuela. In 1828 and 1829 he was largely instrumental in detaching Venezuela from Colombia. He was president of the new republic from 1831

to 1835 and again from 1839 to 1843; from 1860 to 1863 he was dictator; even during those years in which he held no public office he wielded a decisive influence in Venezuelan affairs.

35. QUIROGA, JUAN FACUNDO (1790-1835).—An Argentine soldier, politician, and *caudillo*. His parents were shepherds in the Argentine province of San Juan. During his youth and early manhood he was notorious as a gambler and highway robber; later he became one of the henchmen of the dictator Rosas. His cruelty, unscrupulousness, and reckless daring were proverbial; for a time he was absolute master of the provinces of La Roja and Tucumán. Though for a time he worked in harmony with the government at Buenos Aires, he at length forfeited the confidence of Rosas, and at the latter's instigation was assassinated. Sarmiento has made Quiroga the central figure in his celebrated work, *Facundo Quiroga o civilización y barbarie en las pampas argentinas*, (Buenos Aires, 1852; English translation by Mrs. Horace Mann, London, 1868).

36. MONAGAS, JOSÉ TADEO (1784-1868).—A Venezuelan general and politician, prominent in the affairs of his country from 1835 to 1868. Cf. Dawson, *South American Republics*, II, pp. 384 ff.

37. ALBERDI, JUAN BAUTISTA (1810-1884).—A noted Argentine historian and economist. Among his important works are: *Bases y puntos de partida para la organización política de la Republica Argentina*, (Valparaiso, 1852); *La Republica Argentina consolidada en 1880 con la ciudad de Buenos Aires por capital*, (Buenos Aires, 1881); *Escritos postumos*, (16 vols., Buenos Aires, 1895-1901). Professor Reinsch considers Alberdi as "the most original thinker in politics whom South America has produced," ("The Study of South American History" in *Turner Essays on American History*, New York, 1901, p. 273).

38. ROSAS, JOSÉ MANUEL DE (1793-1877).—Dictator of Buenos Aires. In 1828 he became chief of the Federalist Party in the United Provinces of Buenos Aires in opposition to the so-called Unitarians, and from 1835 to 1852 he was an absolute dictator. This was one of the dark periods in Argentine history. The press was muzzled, commerce was practically at a standstill, the majority of the leading men of the country were assassinated or driven into exile. Though nominally a Federalist, Rosas really put into operation a highly centralized government. He was at length defeated by Urquiza, the governor of the province of Entre Rios, at Monte Caseros near Buenos Aires, on February 3, 1852. He fled to England, where he lived in obscurity until his death. The standard work on this period is that of J. Ramos Mejia, *Rosas y su tiempo*, (Buenos Aires, 1907).

39. FRANCIA, JOSÉ GASPAR RODRIGUEZ (1761-1840).—The famous dictator of Paraguay. From 1814 to 1840 he ruled Paraguay as an absolute despot; during this period Paraguay was practically cut off from the rest of the world. Carlyle has written a brilliant though one-sided defense of "the lonely Francia," depicting him as "a man or sovereign of iron energy and industry, of great and severe labor." The essay originally appeared in the Foreign Quarterly Review for 1843, and is reprinted in his Critical and Miscellaneous Essays. Cf. also *The History of Paraguay*, by C. A. Washburn, (2 vols., New York, 1871).

NOTES ON LECTURE V.

1. BELLO, ANDRES.—Born at Caracas, Venezuela, 1781; died at Santiago, Chile, 1865. A distinguished Spanish American author and scholar. On the outbreak of the Wars of Independence he threw in his lot with the revolutionists, and in 1810 was sent by Bolívar on a diplomatic mission to London, where he resided for nineteen years. In 1834 he accepted a post in the Chilean treasury, took up his residence at Santiago, and was instrumental in founding the University of Santiago (1843), of which he became rector. His literary activity was amazing; he wrote prose works dealing with law, philosophy, literary criticism and philology; of these the best known is his *Grammatica castellaña* (1847). An authority both in Spain and Spanish America, his fame as a poet was won by his *Silvas Americanas,* in which the natural beauties of South America are described with extraordinary charm. He was chiefly responsible for the Chilian law code promulgated in 1855. Bello's complete works in fifteen volumes were published under the auspices of the Chilian government between 1881 and 1893. The standard biography of Bello is that of M. L. Amunátagui, (Santiago de Chile, 1882).

2. MORILLO, PABLO (1777-1838).—A Spanish general, who from 1815 to 1820 attempted to put down the revolution in Venezuela and New Granada. At first successful, he was later outwitted and outgeneraled by Bolívar, by whom in 1829 he was obliged to sign a truce; he was then recalled to Spain at his own request.

3. MORENO, MARIANO (1778-1811).—Argentine lawyer and editor. He studied law at Buenos Aires and in the year 1800 completed his studies in Upper Peru at Chuquisaca. In 1805 he returned to Buenos Aires and at the request of the Argentine land owners drew up the *Representación de los hacendados,* alluded to by Dr. Lima in Lecture VI. He took an active part in the movement looking towards national emancipation, and on May 25, 1810, was appointed secretary general of the first governing "junta." At the same time he was editor of "La Gaceta." As his views conflicted with the president of the Junta, Cornelio Saavedra, he resigned on December 18, 1810. In January 1811 he was appointed the first representative of the new nation to England, but died on his way thither (March 4, 1811). Our chief source for his life and political activity is the biography written by his brother, Manuel Moreno, *Vida y memorias*

del Dr. Mariano Moreno, secretario de la junta de Buenos Aires, (London, 1812; enlarged ed., 1836).

4. GUIBERT, JACQUES ANTOINE HIPPOLYTE, COMTE DE.—A French general and celebrated military writer. His work, *Essai général de tactique*, (Paris, 1770), has been styled the best essay on war produced by any modern writer previous to 1871. The letters of the famous Mlle de Lespinasse (1732-1776) were written to Guibert between 1773 and 1776; they were published in 1809, and have been compared by Sainte Beuve to the Latin Letters of Héloïse to Abelard.

5. OLMEDO, JOSÉ JOAQUIN (1782-1847).—A famous Ecuadorian poet and politician. He played a prominent part in the Wars of Independence; after the creation of the Republic of Ecuador he held various positions of importance and trust up to his death. He is chiefly known outside of Ecuador as a lyric poet; the Pindaric poem referred to by Dr. Lima was published in London in 1826 under the title *La victoria de Junin, canto á Bolívar*.

6. Battle of Ayacucho.—See Lecture IV, notes 11 and 31.

7. CUERVO, RUFENO JOSÉ (1847-1892).—The most important works of this distingished Colombian scholar are: *Apuntos criticos sobre el lenguaje bogantano*, (5th ed., Paris, 1907); *Diccionario de construcción y regimen de la lengua castellaña*, (Paris, 1886); and his edition of Bello's *Grammatica de la Lengua castellaña destinada al uso de los Americanos*, (10th ed., Paris, 1907). Cf. also *Vida de Rufino Cuervo y noticias de su epoca* por Angel y Rufino Cuervo, (Paris, 1892).

8. Congress of Tacumán.—A general congress held in Tacumán in 1816 in order to give a permanent organization to the revolted provinces of the Rio de la Plata. Complete separation from Spain was decreed; the new state took the name of the United Provinces of the Rio de la Plata, and Pueyrredon was chosen "Supreme Director" of the confederation. Cf. Mitre, *Historia de San Martin*, tomo I, *passim*.

9. Assembly of 1823.—This was the famous body summoned by Dom Pedro (later Emperor Dom Pedro I) to draw up a constitution for Brazil. The sessions of this assembly, which began in May 1823, became so stormy, and in the opinion of Dom Pedro so menacing to his authority, that he dissolved it in November of the same year. The constitution which the Assembly drew up was not promulgated. On this subject see Pereira da Silva, *Historia de fundacão do imperio do Brazil*, (Rio de Janeiro, 1864-1868), tomos VI y VII, *passim*; Armitage, *History of Brazil*, (London, 1836), vol. II.

10. GAMARRA ET DAVALOS (JOANNES BENEDICTUS).—The only re-

ference I can find to this priest is the statement that he was the author of *Musa Americana, seu de Deo carmina ad usum scholarum Congregationis S. Philippi Nerii Municipii S. Michaelis in Nova Hispania*, (Gadibus, 1769).

11. The famous Portuguese Constituent Assembly of 1821, brought about by the revolution of the previous year. The treatment accorded the Brazilian deputies by the Portuguese majority was one of the causes of the definite independence of Brazil. On this topic see the able monograph of M. E. Gomez de Carvalho, *Os deputados brasileiros nas cortes geraes de 1821*, (Porto, 1911).

12. See Lecture III, note 35.

13. BLANCO, EDUARDO.—*La Venezuela heroica*, (Caracas, 1881). Other works by this well known Venezuelan author are *El numero III, Vanitas Vanitatum, Una noche en Ferrara*, and *Zarate*.

14. HUAYNA CAPAC.—The Inca who ruled from 1480 to 1523. He was the last ruler to wield undisputed sway over the Inca empire. On his death his sons Huascar and Atahualpa engaged in a bloody civil war which lasted up to the arrival of the Spaniards under Pizarro. The reference in Dr. Lima's lecture is of course to Olmedo's poem "Junin."

15. MERA, JUAN LEON (1832-).—*La virgen del sol, leyenda indiana*, (Quito, 1861). Among the other important works of this author may be mentioned *El heroe marter, Ultimos momentos de Bolívar, La musa perdida, Cartas ineditas de Olmedo*.

16. ALENCAR, JOSÉ MARTINIANO DE (1829-1877).—Among the best known works of this celebrated Brazilian novelist are *O Guarany, Iracema, O Sertanejo*. A brief but admirable appreciation of Alencar may be found in Garcia Merou, *El Bresil intelectual*, (Buenos Aires, 1900). Cf. also Silvio Romero, *Historia de la litteratura brazileira*, (Rio de Janeiro, 1886). For Gonçalves Dias see Lecture II, note 9.

17. VERISSIMO, JOSÉ.—One of the foremost living Brazilian literary critics and educators. His voluminous works include *Estudios de literatura brazileira*, 4 vols.; *Impressiões do Sul; Escenas da vida da Amazonas*, etc. At the present time Dr. Verissimo is director of the Normal school at Rio de Janeiro. Cf. Garcia Merou, *op. cit.*, pp. 97-141.

18. CHOCANO SANTOS.—*Alma America*, (Paris, n. d.). Chief among this poet's other works are *En la aldea, La selva virgin, La epopeya del Pacifico, Fiat lux*.

19. BARBOSA, RUY (1849-).—A distinguished Brazilian statesman, jurist and writer. He played an active part in the political events of the last days of the empire, attracting wide attention by his speeches in the

Brazilian parliament in favor of abolition. On the establishment of the Republic he was minister of finance under the provisional government; during the presidencies of Generals Deodoro da Fonseca and Floriano Peixoto he vigorously attacked the pretorian methods of government in his periodical "O Seculo"; appointed delegate of Brazil at the Second Hague Conference, he distinguished himself by his able championship of the rights of the South American Republic. In 1909 he was nominated for the presideny by the Civil Party, but was defeated by Marshal Hermes da Fonseca. In 1913 he was again nominated for the presidency, this time by the Republican Liberal Party, but withdrew his candidacy in December the same year. At the present time he is Senator from Bahia. The voluminous writings of Ruy Barbosa cover a wide range of topics, from a brilliant criticism of Swift to a plan for the reorganization of the educational system of Brazil. Cf. Garcia Merou, *El Bresil intelectual*, cap. 30-33.

20. See Lecture I, note 29.

21. MORAES SILVA, ANTONIO DE (1757-1825).—The first edition of his *Diccionario da lingua portugueza* appeared in 1789.

22. BLUTEAU, RAPHAEL (1638-1734).—*Diccionario da lingua portugueza*, (Lisboa, 1789).

23. See above, note 7.

24. DARIO, RUBEN.—Among the best known works of this famous Nicaraguan author are *Epistolas y Poemas, Azul, Cantos de Vida y Esperanza; España contemporanea, Tierras solares, Parisiana*. The last three are prose works.

25. GARCIA MORENO, DIEGO.—Born at Guayaquil, 1821; assassinated at Quito, 1875, An Ecuadorian politician; president 1861-65; 1869-75. He was famous for his extreme clerical and ultramontain tendencies; under his rule the government of Ecuador approached a theocracy. He even offered Pius IX an asylum after the abolition of the pope's temporal power. Cf. the eulogistic biography by Father A. Berthe, *Garcia Moreno, Président de l'Equateur*, (Paris, 1888).

26. LAGARRIGUE, JUAN ENRIQUE (1852-).—A noted Chilian Positivist who attempted to effect a partial reconciliation between the philosophy of Comte and the doctrines of Catholicism. His most important works are *La religión de la humanidad*, (Santiago, 1890), and *Hacia la regeneración definitiva*, (Santiago, 1908).

27. For an illuminating discussion of the role of Positivism in the recent history of Brazil see R. Teixeira Mendes, *Benjamin Constant, Esboço de uma appreciação sinthetica da vida e da obra do Fundador da*

Republica Brazileira, (Rio de Janeiro, 1892). Teixeira Mendez is the greatest living authority on Positivism in Brazil. Cf. also Garcia Merou, *op. cit.*, pp. 83-97.

28. BARRETO, TOBIAS (d. 1889).—Barreto's chief work is his *Estudios allemães*, (Rio de Janeiro, 1892). The best short appreciation of the place of this philosopher in the history of Brazilian thought is to be found in Garcia Merou, *op. cit.*, cap. VI.

29. DIAZ RODRIGUEZ, MANUEL.—Among the best known works of this author are *Idolos rotos, Sangre patricia, Confidencias de Psiquis.*

30. NETTO, COELHO.—Among the best known works of this writer are *Miragem, A Esphinge, Apologos, Conferencias litterarias, Scenas e perfis,* etc. For a good brief discussion of the contemporaneous Latin American novel see F. Garcia Calderon, *Les démocraties latines de l'Amérique*, liv. V, ch. ii.

31. Cf. Lecture I, note 22.

NOTES ON LECTURE VI.

1. For the struggle between the Portuguese and the Dutch (1624-1662) see Southey, *History of Brazil*, vol. I, chs. xiv-xvii; Watson, *Spanish and Portuguese America during the Colonial Period*, vol. II, pp. 1 ff.; Edmundson, in *English Historical Review*, vol. XI (1896), 231 ff.; vol. XIV (1899), 676 ff.; vol. XV (1900), 38 ff.; Varnhagen, *Historia geral do Brazil*, (2 vols., Rio de Janeiro, 1854 and 1857).

2. PÉTION, ALEXANDRE (1770-1818).—President of Haiti from 1807 to 1818. For an account of his relations with Bolívar, who was an exile in Haiti from January to March, 1816, see F. L. Petrie, *Simon Bolivar*, (New York, 1899).

3. ZUMETA, CARLOS (CESAR).—*El continente enfermo*, (New York, 1899).

4. PRADT, ABBÉ DE.—This is the well known Dufour de Pradt, Bishop of Poitiers, and later Archbishop of Mechlin. De Pradt's reflections on Latin America are found in his *Des colonies et de la révolution actuelle de l'Amérique*, (Paris, 1817).

5. See Lecture IV, note 20.

6. War of the Pacific (1879-1883).—The struggle between Chile and Peru—the latter aided by Bolivia—for the possession of the rich nitrate and guano deposits belonging to Bolivia and Peru. The war resulted in a decisive victory for Chile. Cf. Sir Clements Markham, *The War between Chile and Peru*, (London, 1882), and Diego Barros Arana, *Histoire de la guerre du Pacifique*, (Paris, 1881).

7. GAUCHO.—The name given to the cow-boys or riders of the vast pampas or plains of Argentine and Uruguay. The *gauchos*, though generally of Spanish descent, have become a distinct type, which, however, is fast disappearing before the march of civilization.

8. See Lecture I, note 15.

9. LLANERO.—The name applied to the inhabitants of the vast plains or llanos of Venezuela. The llaneros possess many of the characteristics of the *gauchos*, but are apt to be more turbulent and warlike. On several occasions they played a decisive part in the Venezuelan Wars of Independence.

10. See Lecture I, note 3.

11. See Lecture I, note 22.

12. See Lecture IV, note 34.

13. SANTANDER, FRANCISCO DE PAULA (1792-1840).—A prominent South American general and statesman, frequently spoken of as the founder of the Republic of New Granada. Though he had coöperated with Bolívar in the Wars of Independence, he came into conflict with him on the question of Greater Colombia; there is even some evidence that Santander was involved in an attempt to assassinate Bolívar shortly before the latter's death. On the disintegration of Greater Colombia, Santander was elected President of New Granada (1832), an office he held until 1837. For Paez, cf. Lecture IV, note 34.

14. See Lecture IV, note 38.

15. PORTALES, DIEGO JOSÉ VICTOR (1793-1837).—A Chilian politician and leader of the Conservative Party. Though Portales never held any higher position than Minister of War and Vice-President (1830-31; 1835-37), he largely shaped the policies of the Conservative Party and helped to lay the foundation of their power, which lasted until 1861. While refusing to allow the mass of the people any active participation in the government, the Conservative leaders devoted themselves to improving the conditions of the people, and under their highly centralized rule Chile advanced rapidly in prosperity.

16. Cf. Garcia Calderon, *Les démocraties latines*, liv. II.

17. CASTILLA, RAMON (1796-1867).—President of Peru from 1845 to 1851 and from 1855 to 1862. Under Castilla, Peru enjoyed an era of great progress and prosperity.

18. See Lecture IV, note 39.

19. SANTA ANNA, ANTONIO LOPEZ DE (1795-1876).—The famous Mexican general and politician, prominent in the affairs of his country from 1821 to 1856.

20. GUZMAN BLANCO, ANTONIO (1828-1889).—A Venezuelan soldier and politician, known by his admirers as the "Illustrious American." From 1863 to 1888 he directly or indirectly controlled the government of Venezuela. During his various presidential terms he adorned the cities of Caracas with many fine buildings and statues of himself. The vagaries of this eccentric though in some respects able man are described by W. E. Curtiss in his *Venezuela*, (New York, 1896).

21. MALGAREJO, MARIANO (1818-1872).—A Bolivian general and revolutionist. His tenure of power in Bolivia was accompanied by a long series of assassinations and disorders; he represents the most odious type of a revolutionary despot, masquerading under the trappings of republicanism. Characteristic examples of Malgarejo's conduct are given by Prince Louis d'Orleans Bragance in his interesting work, *Sous la croix du sud*, (Paris, 1912), ch. xviii.

22. See Lecture V, note 25.

23. CLEMENCEAU.—*Notes de voyage dans l'Amérique du sud*, (Paris, 1911), ch. vii.

24. ALAMAN, *Historia de Mexico*, (5 vols., Mexico, 1849). *Noticia preliminar*.

25. Tupis.—The Tupi stock included a considerable portion of the aborigines of Brazil, especially those inhabiting the littoral and the lower Amazon Valley. The Tupis were closely related to the Guaranys of Paraguay. The language spoken by these two groups was known by the Portuguese as the *lingua geral*, a sort of *lingua franca*, generally understood throughout Brazil and Paraguay. Cf. D. G. Brinton, *The American Race*, (Philadelphia, 1901), pp. 229-236.

26. Buccan.—A native Caribbean word originally applied to a wooden rack or frame on which meat was smoked or dried by the Caribs; later the term was applied to meat thus prepared. The word "buccaneer" is derived from *buccan*.

27. See Lecture I, note 4.

28. See Lecture I, note 15.

29. The Paraguayan War (1865-1870).—This war had for its object the overthrow of the Paraguayan dictator Lopez by the combined forces of Brazil, Argentina and Uruguay. The result was the complete prostration of Paraguay and the killing off of the larger part of her male population. Of the numerous works on this subject perhaps the most interesting is that of Richard F. Burton, *Letters from the Battlefields of Paraguay*, (London, 1870).

30. See Lecture V, note 3.

31. The Chilian constitution of 1833, which with certain modifications remains the constitution of Chile at the present time, provided for a highly centralized government based on a small electorate. It was by means of this instrument that the Conservatives maintained themselves in power from 1830 to 1861.

32. Here, of course, Dr. Lima refers to the "Valorization Plan of 1906." The best discussion of this extraordinary economic experiment is that furnished by Pierre Denis, in *Le Brésil au XXe siècle*, ch. ix, (Paris, 1910; English translation, London, 1911).

33. Dr. Lima refers, I think, to the work of Arthur Ruhl, *The Other Americans*, (New York, 1908). An illuminating discussion of this "realistic tone" in Argentine letters will be found in the essay of Professor Paul Reinsch, "Some Notes on the Study of South American History," in the *Turner Essays on American History*, (New York, 1910).

34. CLEMENCEAU, *Notes de voyage*, ch. xii.
35. Cf. Lecture V, note 19.
36. TRIANA, SANTIAGO PEREZ (1859-).—Well known Colombian writer and politician. At the Second Hague Conference, in conjunction with General Jorge Holguin, he advanced the doctrine that each of the Signatory Powers of the Hague Convention, or Treaty, shall agree not to make war upon any other without having had recourse to the Hague Tribunal. Among his best known works are *The International Position of the Latin American Races* in Cambridge Modern History, (New York, 1910), vol. XII, p. 690-702, and *Down the Orinoco in a Canoe*, (New York, 1902).
37. DRAGO, LUIS MARIA (1859-).—Noted Argentine writer and statesman. He first attained international prominence by his note of December 29, 1902, to Secretary Hay in reference to the Venezuelan crisis. In this he contended that no collection of government bonds ought to provoke armed intervention and still less territorial occupation. This same doctrine, subsequently known as the Drago Doctrine, was advanced, though unsuccessfully, at the Hague Conference of 1907.
38. Among the many accounts of the marvelous work of Dr. Oswaldo Cruz in the sanitation of Rio de Janeiro, that by Paul Walle in his work, *Au Brésil de l'Uruguay au Rio São Francisco*, (Paris, n. d.), ch. i, is perhaps the most satisfactory in a small compass.
39. SARMIENTO, DOMINGO FAUSTINO (1811-1888).—A distinguished Argentine statesman, educator and author, frequently called the "School-Master President of Argentina." He was appointed minister of public instruction in 1860 and minister of the interior in 1861, and while minister to the United States was elected president of the Argentine Republic for the term 1868-1874. His great work was the improvement and extension of popular education; in this achievement he derived great advantage from his sojourn and studies in the United States. For a brief appreciation of the life and work of Sarmiento see the article by F. N. Noa, *Sarmiento, Statesman and Educator*, in the Arena, vol. XXXVI, pp. 390-395 (October 1906). Further particulars are given in the Biography of Sarmiento by Mrs. Horace Mann, incorporated in her translation of Sarmiento's most famous work, *Facundo*, or *Civilization and Barbarism*, (London, 1868).
40. This idea is further developed in Dr. Lima's *Pan-Americanismo, Bolivar-Monroe-Roosevelt*, (Paris, 1908).
41. DR. ROQUE SAENZ-PENA.—Inaugurated 1910. An account of the previous career of President Saenz-Peña will be found in Blasco Ibañez, *Argentina y sus grandezas*, (Madrid, n. d.), pp. 334 *et seq.*

www.ingramcontent.com/pod-product-compliance
Lightning Source LLC
Chambersburg PA
CBHW031421290426
44110CB00011B/470